Believe

as Jesus Believed

BOOK 1 EXPERIENCE THE LIFE

Believe
as Jesus Believed

with Leader's Guide and DVD

Transformed Mind

BILL HULL & PAUL MASCARELLA

NavPress is the publishing ministry of The Navigators, an international Christian organization and leader in personal spiritual development. NavPress is committed to helping people grow spiritually and enjoy lives of meaning and hope through personal and group resources that are biblically rooted, culturally relevant, and highly practical.

For a free catalog go to www.NavPress.com
or call 1.800.366.7788 in the United States or 1.800.839.4769 in Canada.

ISBN-13: 978-1-61521-540-9

Cover design by Arvid Wallen
Cover image by Shutterstock

Printed in the United States of America

1 2 3 4 5 6 7 8 / 14 13 12 11 10

CONTENTS

INTRODUCTION

To *experience the life* is to commit to a way or pattern of life. Its basis is humility and it is a life of self-denial and submission to others. The life that Jesus lived and prescribed for us is different from the one being offered by many churches. His servant leadership was radically distinct from what is extolled by secular society and even too bold for what is modeled in the Christian community. This life is essentially the *faith of following*, of taking up one's cross daily and following Him. It is fundamentally about giving up the right to run your own life. It is living the life that Jesus lived, the life to which He has called every disciple.

To put it another way, we can only experience the life Jesus has called us to by committing to:

- Believe as Jesus believed
- Live as Jesus lived
- Love as Jesus loved
- Minister as Jesus ministered
- Lead as Jesus led

Will we choose to live as Jesus lived, to follow Him regardless of where He leads? Or will we surrender to the powerful forces of our culture, incorporate its corrupting values, and adopt its devaluing methods into our pursuit of God? To do the latter is simply to begin by failing. A faith which can accommodate both the world's values and its methods is not the faith to which Jesus calls us. It is not the faith which is the "victory that has overcome the world" (1 John 5:4). It is a faith which is being overcome by the world. It is only by experiencing the life that Jesus lived that we will "find rest for [our] souls" (Matthew 11:28-29).

ABOUT THIS BOOK

Its Purpose

EXPERIENCE THE LIFE exists to assist the motivated disciple in entering into a more profound way of thinking and living. That way is the pattern of life Jesus modeled and then called every interested person to follow. Simply put, it is the living out of Jesus' life by believing as Jesus believed, living as Jesus lived, loving as Jesus loved, ministering as Jesus ministered, and leading as Jesus led. This *Life* is a life grounded in humility—characterized by submission, obedience, suffering, and the joys of exaltation. It is the life that transforms its adherents and penetrates the strongest resistance. It then calls upon each person to rethink what it means to be a follower of Jesus.

This book is the first in the five-book EXPERIENCE THE LIFE series.[1] It is designed to lead disciples in a thirty-week course, built upon the ideas introduced and developed in Bill Hull's book *Choose the Life.* It provides a daily format which directs a disciple's thinking toward the application of these truths, thereby producing in him a faith hospitable to healthy spiritual transformation—*a faith that embraces discipleship.*

Its Participants

Virtually all significant change can, should be, and eventually is tested in relationship to others. To say that one is more loving without it being verified in relation to others is hollow. Not only do others need to be involved to test one's progress, they are needed to encourage and help

1. If you are joining an Experience the Life community that has already completed the first week in the ETL course (Book One: *Believe as Jesus Believed,* Week One) follow the instructions found in Appendix Two.

someone else in the journey of transformation. Therefore, going on the journey with others is absolutely necessary.

The five books are designed to lead each disciple in a personal journey of spiritual formation by his participation within a community of disciples, who have likewise decided to *experience the life*.

The community is composed of (optimally) from two to eight disciples being led in this thirty-week course to *experience the life*.

Participants in the community agree to make time and perform the daily assignments as directed in each book. They have agreed to pray daily for the other members of their community and to keep whatever is shared at their community meeting in confidence. They will attend and fully participate in each weekly community meeting.

Its Process

We recognize that all change, all spiritual transformation, is the result of a process. Events may instigate change in people; they may provide the motive, the occasion, and the venue for change to begin, but the changes that result in healthy spiritual transformation are the product of a process.

We can glean a description of the transformational process from the apostle Paul's command in Romans 12:2:

> Do not conform any longer to the pattern of this world, but be transformed by the renewing of your mind. Then you will be able to test and approve what God's will is—his good, pleasing and perfect will.

This process of transformation asserts that the believer must no longer conform to what is false, the "pattern of this world" (its ideas and values, and the behaviors which express them). Also, he must be transformed, which means his pattern must be changed, conformed to another pattern (the truth), which is not "of this world." This is done by the process of "the renewing of your mind." What does it mean to renew something? To what is Paul referring when he says that the mind must undergo this renewal?

To renew something means to act upon something in ways that will cause it to be as it was when it was new. The principle idea is one of restoring something that is currently malfunctioning and breaking down to its fully functioning state, its original pristine state, the state it was in prior to it sustaining any damage. We must avoid the modern notion that renewing something means simply replacing the old thing with an entirely new thing. Paul, and the people to whom he wrote these words, would simply not understand *renew* to mean anything like what we moderns mean when we use the word *replace*. They would understand that renewing the wheels on one's cart meant repairing them to their fully functioning state. And so, what Paul means by "being transformed by the *renewing* of your mind" (emphasis added) is that the mind must undergo changes, repairs that will restore it to its original condition, the fully functioning state it enjoyed when it was first created. As these repairs proceed in the restoration/renewal process and a detrimental modification to the original design is discovered, that modification must be removed. It must be removed so that it will not interfere with its operating as it was originally designed. Further, to properly renew anything, we must understand its original design. The best way to renew something is with the direction and assistance of the original builder. A builder in Paul's day was not only the builder but also the designer and architect. With the expertise and help available through the builder, full renewal is best accomplished.

If you are renewing a house, that house's builder would best know how to go about it. If you are renewing an automobile, that automobile's builder would best know how to go about it. In our case, we are renewing the mind. It stands to reason then that its renewal would best be accomplished in partnership with its Architect/Builder—God.

We know that it is the mind that is to be renewed, and that we should partner with God to accomplish its renewal, but what is it about the mind that is being renewed? Is it broken, in need of new parts?

When Paul says that it is the mind which is being renewed when spiritual transformation is taking place, he means much more than what most of us think of when we use the word *mind*. Most of us think of the mind as some sort of calculator in our head, so it's understandable that our idea of renewing it would start with the idea of replacing its broken parts. But for Paul, the mind is much more than a calculator in our head, and to renew it means more than simply swapping out a sticky key, or a cracked screen, or replacing the batteries that have run low.

The Greek word that Paul uses and is translated as the English word *mind* is νους. Here it means the inner direction of one's thoughts and will and the orientation of one's moral consciousness. When Paul refers to our mind's renewal, he is saying that the current direction of our thoughts and will must be changed. The way our mind currently directs our thoughts and will no longer leads to where the mind was originally designed to take our thoughts and will. Our mind no longer leads our thinking to know the will of God, to know what is good, pleasing, and perfect, and no longer directs our will to accomplish God's will, to do what is good, pleasing, and perfect. This is in large part what is meant by being lost. If our minds are not renewed, then we cannot live a life directed toward doing what is pleasing to God. We need to undergo the restoration process that will return our minds to operating as they were originally designed, allowing our minds to direct our thinking and will toward God. The good news is that the original Builder/Architect—God—prescribed the renewing of the mind as the sure remedy to restoring us to spiritual health, and He intends to partner with us in this restoration process.

For spiritual transformation to occur there must be a partnership between the Holy Spirit and the person who is to undergo transformation. It is good news that the Holy Spirit is involved in the process of our restoration because, unlike other things that undergo restoration, like houses, tables, and chairs, we are not just passive things. We are more. We are *beings*, *human* beings, *made* in the image of God. Being made in the image of God includes much more than I will (or even can) mention, but for our purposes it includes having thoughts, ideas, passions, desires, and a will of our own. Because these abilities in their current condition (i.e., before renewal) no longer lead us toward God's will, we do not have the ability to direct our own transformation. We need someone who is not "conformed to the pattern of this world," one who is completely conformed to the will of God, to direct the renewal. And because we are in this prerenewal condition, we need someone to initiate, to enable us, and encourage us to continue the process, someone who is not subject to the same problems our condition allows. Who is better to direct than God? Who is better to enable and encourage than God? There is none better suited to the task than the Holy Spirit. That we are partnering with Him is good news indeed!

With the initiating, enabling, and direction of the Holy Spirit, the process of renewal can begin. It is a two-stage process: the *appropriation of the truth* and the *application of truth-directed behavior*. The first stage, the *appropriation of the truth*, takes place when:

1. we have the desire to pursue the Truth to be changed;
2. we then act upon that desire, choosing to pursue the Truth by setting our will.

The second stage, the *application of truth-directed behavior*, takes place when:

1. we begin practicing behaviors, which we'll describe as spiritual disciplines, designed to halt our conformity to "the pattern of this world";
2. we engage in transformational activities, which are designed to reorient our mind and direct it toward God's will;
3. we continue to practice transformational activities to introduce and establish new patterns of thinking and behavior which conforms our mind to the mind of Christ.

The same components in the process for renewing the mind that we gleaned from the apostle Paul can also be seen in Jesus' call to anyone who would follow Him.

Jesus commanded to all who would follow Him (i.e., all disciples) to:

> Come to me, all you who are weary and burdened, and I will give you rest. Take my yoke upon you and learn from me, for I am gentle and humble in heart, and you will find rest for your souls. (Matthew 11:28-29)

Jesus begins with a promise, "Come . . . and I will give you rest." He kindles a desire to follow Him. This is the first step in *the appropriation of truth*, the *desire* to pursue the Truth. We *desire* change. Next is Jesus' command to take His yoke. This is the second step in the *appropriation of truth*, *choosing* to pursue the truth. We set our *will* to change. At this step, we can choose to pursue our desire for the truth and change or ignore it. If we choose to delay placing it upon our shoulders, it is at the cost of rest to our souls. The choice precedes the action. Next, we read that we are to take His yoke.

To take His yoke is the first step of the second stage in the process of renewing the mind, the *application of truth-directed behavior*. At this step, as we saw before with Paul, we discontinue with our current ways, which conform us to the pattern of this world. We intentionally begin to dislodge the destructive patterns which have grown in us as a precursor to the second step, the taking-upon of a new way, God's way, His yoke.

The second step, the taking-upon of Jesus' yoke, is the part of the process of renewing the mind where the vacancy left from dislodging our old ways, "the pattern of this world," is being filled up with the new life-giving patterns by which we are to conform our lives. It is this yoke, God's new way of living the life that Jesus lived, that is to be taken upon us. Just as placing a yoke upon the ox's body enables it to perform according to its master's desires and accomplish work it alone would never be able to do, so also Jesus' yoke must be placed upon our body to allow it to perform our Master's work, the renewing of our mind (work we would otherwise not be able to accomplish).

Finally, we see the third and last step in the *application of truth-directed behavior*. This is the final step in the process of renewal, but it is also the beginning step in the ongoing process of our spiritual transformation. It finally brings us all the way to our taking Jesus' yoke upon us. It also begins the continuing journey of knowing and doing God's good, pleasing, and perfect will. While the second step trains the mind through establishing patterns, the third step lives out the new character that has replaced the old. This continuing journey begins once we take His yoke upon us. For then we begin to "learn from me [Jesus]" and thereby experience rest for our soul. This rest, this peacefulness that comes from learning from Jesus, is what it is to live with a renewed mind. It is experiencing the Spirit initiated, encouraged, enabled, and empowered life Jesus enjoyed with the peace that comes only by having the "mind of Christ" and by accomplishing His good, pleasing, and perfect will.

EXPERIENCE THE LIFE provides the disciple a structured process whereby he can engage in the process of spiritual renewal. It provides a daily regimen for practicing specific disciplines designed to displace those old destructive ideas and behaviors (i.e., the patterns of the world) and replace them with new, constructive, life-giving ideas and behaviors (i.e., the mind of Christ).

EXPERIENCE THE LIFE requires commitment to consistently practice the disciplines and to reserve the time required for transformation.

Most studies on change agree that displacing a current habit or idea and establishing a new one requires a minimum of about three months. Also, learning studies demonstrate the necessity of consistent application of the thing being learned to ensure its permanent retention.

According to a leading learning researcher, people remember:

- 10% of what they read
- 20% of what they hear
- 30% of what they see
- 50% of what they see and hear
- 70% of what they say
- 95% of what they teach someone else[2]

---

2. William Glassner, *Control Therapy in the Classroom* (New York: Harper and Row, 1986); *Reality Therapy: A New Approach to Psychiatry* (New York: Harper and Row, 1965).

Simply put, we learn best not by passively hearing and seeing, but by actively "doing" the thing that we are learning.

The most relevant question a teacher can ask is, "Are my students learning?" For our purposes, the relevant question must be, "Am I engaged in a process that will result in my being changed from what I am into what I am to be? Am I being transformed into the image of Christ?"

Each book in this series provides a solid opportunity for significant transformation through the use of several common tools or disciplines, including:

- Reading Scripture together
- Reading a common philosophy of the Christian experience
- Journaling insights, questions, and prayers
- Discussion over material that has already been studied, prayed over, and reflected upon
- Accountability for the purpose of helping each other keep their commitments to God
- Encouragement to help each other overcome areas of defeat and break free from bondage
- Mutual commitment to apply what God has impressed on each member
- Mutual commitment to impact those with whom they have contact

Its Pattern

This course leads the believer to *experience the life* Jesus lived, utilizing a daily regimen to practice the various spiritual disciplines. The course is thirty weeks long over five books.

The five books, each six weeks in length, instruct and challenge the disciples to conform their life to:

1. Believe as Jesus believed
2. Live as Jesus lived
3. Love as Jesus loved

4. Minister as Jesus ministered
5. Lead as Jesus led

Each six-week book leads disciples through a course of daily teachings and exercises in an examination of how Jesus lived out His faith.

In daily sessions, the disciple begins with a prayer focused on the issues to be presented in the daily reading. The daily reading gives a core thought that will be explored in the day's exercises. Questions are designed to help the disciple's understanding of the core thoughts and key ideas. Disciples are then directed to reflect on the application of these core thoughts and key ideas to their own spiritual growth. Journaling space is provided for answering questions and recording thoughts, questions, applications, and insights stemming from their reflection.

Once weekly (the sixth session), the disciple meets with others who comprise their community. At the community meeting they pray together, discuss the core thoughts and key ideas introduced in the week's readings, and share from their own experience of practicing the week's spiritual discipline. They view and discuss the video introduction for the following week's study and pray and encourage one another in their journey of spiritual transformation.

Although the books were designed primarily for use by groups consisting of two to six members, the material and the format can easily be used to effectively lead larger groups in a discussion-based exploration of spiritual transformation.

Lastly, we recommend that the leaders of the weekly discussion groups proceed through each book together as a community group prior to leading their own group. The insights that they will acquire from their own journey through Experience the Life will be invaluable to them and the larger group they will lead.

When leading a larger group through Experience the Life, keep in mind that most of the spiritual traction for transformation is due to the interaction that the Lord has with each individual through the other individuals in a community of believers. To preserve this traction, the leader must provide a venue and time for this interaction. For this reason, we suggest that some time during the weekly session the leader divide the large group into smaller groups mimicking the two- to eight-member community group for the purpose of more intimately discussing the issues presented in the week's session. It is reported after experiencing successive weeks with the same members of this smaller discussion group individuals previously not participants in a small-group program have desired to continue in such a program.

While we believe that the most effective and efficient means of leading individuals to healthy spiritual transformation is in the context of a smaller community group, we do acknowledge that the larger group setting may be the only means currently available to a church's leadership. Though the *form* of instruction is important, the *function* is what must be preserved: *Verum supremus vultus* (truth above form).

Its Product

Each session is designed to challenge the disciple to examine the progress of his own transformation, to train him with the desire to both know God's will and do it. This course values the spiritual traction the disciple can get by facing this challenge in a high-trust community. Christ was a Man for others. Disciples then are to be people for others. It is only in losing ourselves in the mission of loving others that we live in balance and experience the joy that Christ has promised. And therein lie many of the rewards a disciple may enjoy as he lives and loves as Jesus. This is the life that cultivates Christlikeness and whose product is a transformed disciple—the only life of faith worthy of justifying our calling upon others to Experience the Life.

WEEK 1

Redrawing Your Brain Map

DAY ONE

Prayer

Dear Lord, I begin today by boldly admitting to You what You surely already know: that very often what I say and do reveals that I have not truly accepted You as my only Lord. I have not truly believed the truth about You or me. But this day, I choose to be Your disciple. Now, please begin to teach me afresh what I need to know and do, that You may fully enjoy me, and I You. Amen.

Core Thought

Change is a choice, and choosing is changing.

C. S. Lewis wrote:

> People often think of Christian morality as a kind of bargain in which God says, "If you keep a lot of rules I'll reward you, and if you don't I'll do the other thing." I do not think that is the best way of looking at it. I would much rather say that every time you make a choice you are turning the central part of you, the part of you that chooses, into something a little different from what it was before. And taking your life as a whole, with all your innumerable choices, all your life long you are slowly turning this central thing either into a heavenly creature or into a hellish creature: either into a creature that

> is in harmony with God, and with other creatures, and with itself, or else into one that is in a state of war and hatred with God, and with its fellow-creatures, and with itself. To be the one kind of creature is heaven: that is, it is joy and peace, and knowledge and power. To be the other means madness, horror, idiocy, rage, impotence, and eternal loneliness. Each of us at each moment is progressing to the one state or the other.[1]

Today's Exercises

Core Scripture: Romans 12:1-2

Read aloud Romans 12:1-2.

Recite this week's memory verses aloud five times.

> Therefore, I urge you, brothers, in view of God's mercy, to offer your bodies as living sacrifices, holy and pleasing to God—this is your spiritual act of worship. Do not conform any longer to the pattern of this world, but be transformed by the renewing of your mind. Then you will be able to test and approve what God's will is—his good, pleasing and perfect will.

Discovering the Discipline: Lectio Divina

What is Lectio Divina?

Lectio Divina (LD) is one method of practicing the spiritual discipline of biblical meditation. It is a method for reading (Lt. *lectio*) for purposes divine (Lt. *divina*).

We read all kinds of things for different purposes, like comics for entertainment, textbooks to prepare for testing, and cookbooks for meal preparation. In other words, we *use* the things we read to *do something we want done.* Normally, reading is a way we obtain something that we desire having, like a good laugh, or a new technique of accomplishing a task. Most often we read the Bible the same way we read other writings. We usually read the Bible to obtain something we desire

---

1. C. S. Lewis, *Mere Christianity* (New York: Macmillan, 1952), 72.

from its contents, such as learning how I should act or what faith means or enjoying its stories, or sometimes simply to engage in reading itself (e.g., it helps me to fall asleep at night).

LD is different from normal reading because the purpose for which it is used is the opposite of normal reading. Where the purpose of normal reading methods is to accomplish the reader's goals, the purpose of LD's method is to accomplish the *Author's* goals whether the reader shares the author's goals or not. Further, LD differs because it requires a reader to regard its material differently from other reading material.

Unlike other reading material, LD recognizes that what is being read (Holy Scripture, God's Word) is the means by which God the Father engages us. We encounter Him when we interact with Him through interacting with His Word. By practicing LD, we are training ourselves to think and act as if we were actually in the immediate presence of our God, the Father who longs for us to remain near Him always, and interact with Him, having a conversation with Him. It changes reading and knowing things *about* Jesus into knowing Jesus Himself because you have been with Him.

LD assumes that it is impossible for us to become or desire what we have never in the least experienced. LD provides a method of meditating upon God's Word where we come to know God by being with Him as He opens our minds and teaches us and reveals to us the content of our hearts and heals us.

Through this daily meeting with Him, we become renewed in our minds and refreshed from being in the presence of the One who truly loves us beyond our present ability to comprehend.

Tomorrow we will explore the first of *Lectio Divina's* four elements of divine reading. For now, reread Romans 12:1–2, asking God to prepare you to learn and practice the spiritual discipline of meditation via *Lectio Divina*.

Reflections

What would you expect to experience as you are meditating via *Lectio Divina* in the very presence of Jesus?

we each must choose to
look at + Reflect upon scripture
as more Then words - as divine
words written directly to me

Prayer

Pray for each member of your community.

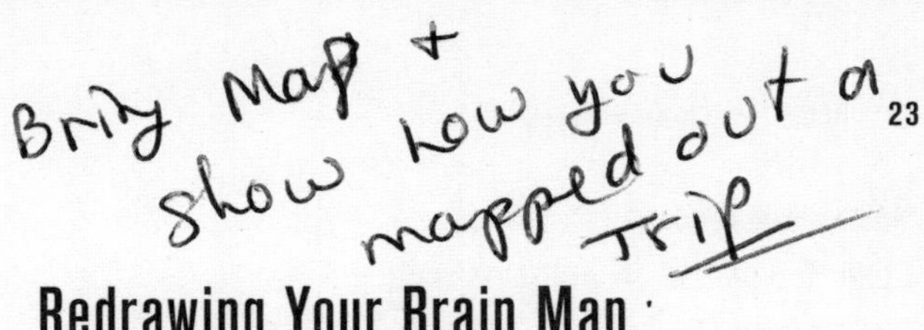

Redrawing Your Brain Map

DAY TWO

Prayer

Dear Lord, help me to continually ask You what Your will is for me today, not to know what to do next, necessarily, but to know what is most important to You. If I know what is most important to You, then I will be present and ready to do what You want done and not so easily distracted by all the things I think are urgent. Amen.

Core Thought

Change is choosing a new mental map.

Individual change starts and ends with the mental maps people carry in their heads.[2] Just as actual maps guide the steps of travelers, mental maps direct people's behavior. If a person's mental map does not change, he will not change. Therefore, change must focus on individuals redrawing their mental maps.

The apostle Paul said it so well: "Do not be conformed any longer to the pattern of this world, but be transformed by the *renewing of the mind*. Then [an often forgotten caveat] you will be able to test and approve what God's will is—his good, pleasing and perfect will" (Romans 12:2, emphasis added).

The proof of a renewed mind is testing your new ideas in the crucible of daily experience. This implies that without the process of renewing the mind, a person cannot and will not test and approve God's will. He can neither know His will, nor live it.

2. Mental map concept based on *Leading Strategic Change: Breaking Through the Brain Barrier* by J. Stewart Black and Hal B. Gregersen (Upper Saddle River, NJ: Prentice Hall, 2003).

Today's Exercises

Core Scripture: Romans 12:1-2

Read aloud Romans 12:1-2.

Recite this week's memory verses aloud five times.

> Therefore, I urge you, brothers, in view of God's mercy, to offer your bodies as living sacrifices, holy and pleasing to God—this is your spiritual act of worship. Do not conform any longer to the pattern of this world, but be transformed by the renewing of your mind. Then you will be able to test and approve what God's will is—his good, pleasing and perfect will.

Discovering the Discipline: Lectio Divina

Lectio Divina–the Four Elements of Divine Reading

Yesterday, we learned that *Lectio Divina* (LD) is one method of practicing the spiritual discipline of biblical meditation. *Lectio Divina* provides a method of meditating upon God's Word where we come to know God by becoming present with God and interacting with Him. LD consists of four elements or steps for divine reading (that is, for reading to accomplish the divine purpose of meditating upon God's Word): *Read it*, *Think it*, *Pray it*, and *Live it*. Today, we will learn and practice the first element, *Read it*.

Read It

LD begins by practicing the first element called *Read it*. This kind of reading is a specialized reading method. It attempts to recover the feel of spoken narrative from written prose. *Lectio* requires that we always keep in mind the idea that language is first and foremost a spoken means of communication. When we read Scripture we are three steps removed from experiencing the text as it was originally communicated. Unlike its original hearers we hear it in our time, in our place, with our cultural perspective. Because of this, we must read in a special way to overcome this removal. The sentences we read on paper were first spoken (at least heard in the author's head, spoken by the mind's voice). It is only after being spoken and heard that they could be written to read. Reading is actually an attempt to re-create the spoken, real-time communication of living beings from written letters and numbers. Generally speaking, one can see there is the possibility that much meaning can be lost in the process of speech becoming writing, the writing being read, and reading re-creating the original speech. Fortunately, Holy Scripture does not suffer a loss of meaning due to its having been spoken first and then committed to writing. The Holy Spirit has preserved its accuracy by superintending this process. However, this does not preclude our misunderstanding what the Holy Spirit has written. *Read it* helps overcome some of our misunderstanding by resurrecting to life the original speech that is captured in the writings of Holy Scripture.

Read it captures the life in the text by asking the reader to become a listener to the speech, hearing in it the original passion with which it was spoken. It declares that we must truly hear the Scriptures to read the Scriptures properly. Our goal is to understand it as it was heard by those who first experienced its communication. Scripture is to be understood first in the living context in which it was first received. Therefore, it is imperative that we hear only what the Scriptures have said. To do so means that we must begin by reading only what is in the biblical text. We must guard as much as possible against importing the influence of our time, place, and values, listening to their noises instead of hearing God voice. In *Read it*, we establish what was said and what was heard, we read only what is there, and we train ourselves to hear it how it was heard.

Tomorrow we will explore the next of *Lectio Divina's* four elements of divine reading: *Think it*.

Doing the Discipline: Lectio Divina

Today, you will practice the spiritual discipline of meditating on God's Word using *Lectio Divina*. Usually, all four elements of LD (*Read it, Think it, Pray it,* and *Live it*) are done each day during biblical meditation; next week, you will begin to do exactly that. However, this week you will learn and then practice only one of the steps each day, beginning today with *Read it*. Begin your time of meditation by asking the Holy Spirit to awaken your heart and mind to God's presence. Be sure to end your time of meditation by thanking the Lord for what He is doing in you.

Request to Be in His presence

"Dear Lord, bring me into the context of Your world."

Read it—start by reading Romans 12:1-2 at least twice, slowly, out loud.

Remember: We read now only what is there, to hear once again, *only what was spoken then.* As you read, seek to become conscious of any ideas, notions, or preconceptions that may contaminate your understanding of the passages. For example, "I urge you, brothers" doesn't mean that the apostle intends this to apply only to male believers and not also to female believers.

List those "contaminating" ideas, notions, or preconceptions below.

Give Thanks to the Lord

"Thank You, Lord, for what You are doing in me and for what You want to accomplish in this world through me."

Prayer

Pray for each member of your community.

Redrawing Your Brain Map

DAY THREE

Prayer

Dear Lord, please help me from having a mind so fixed that it resists the changes You wish to make in my beliefs. Help me to become the kind of disciple who so values Your beliefs that I would look forward with excitement when I sense that You are about to shift my understanding toward the Truth. Lord, today I unlock the treasury of all my treasured beliefs. I offer it for use in Your service. Take or leave what You want anytime You will for I am leaving the key with You. Amen.

Core Thought

Change is crashing through the brain barriers.

Hernán Cortés, the Spanish explorer, sailed up the Gulf of California or what we now call the Baja Peninsula. Provisions ran low, the crew grew nervous, and they were forced to turn back. They didn't finish; thus, they could only conclude that California was an island. Later expeditions provided clear proof that California was not an island, but it took two hundred years for a new map to be created.

It is human nature to want to continue to believe what you have come to firmly believe even though new evidence proves it untrue. Remember, it will take time to change from trusting the old beliefs into trusting the new beliefs, but these brain barriers must be toppled before the Truth that God reveals can take its rightful place of prominence in our beliefs.

Today's Exercises

Core Scripture: Romans 12:1-2.

Read aloud Romans 12:1-2.

Recite this week's memory verses aloud five times.

> Therefore, I urge you, brothers, in view of God's mercy, to offer your bodies as living sacrifices, holy and pleasing to God — this is your spiritual act of worship. Do not conform any longer to the pattern of this world, but be transformed by the renewing of your mind. Then you will be able to test and approve what God's will is — his good, pleasing and perfect will.

Discovering the Discipline: Lectio Divina

Think It

Today, we will learn and practice the second element in RSR, *Think it.* Here we meditate upon the text. When we move from *Read it* to *Think it,* "we move from looking at the *words* of the text to entering the *world* of the text."[3] When we meditate upon Scripture, we bring the world where God is revealing Himself into us. Meditation lets the images and stories by which God is revealing Himself penetrate our understanding. But meditation is not a passive engagement.

Meditation is an active engagement that requires participation. In *Think it* "we make ourselves at home and conversant with everyone in the story."[4] *Think it* takes us from forming an understanding of the context to our understanding being formed *within* the context. In biblical meditation, the most comprehensive context will always be centered upon Jesus.

To understand anything within God's Scriptures, we must understand it as it is related to Jesus, for He is the One who has made all things. It follows that to understand ourselves and how we are related to God and all the things of this world and the next, we must understand how we are related to Jesus.

---

3. Eugene Peterson, *Eat This Book* (Grand Rapids, MI: Eerdmans, 2006), 99.

4. Peterson,, 102.

In *Think it,* we discern the connections and listen for the harmonies that come together in Jesus. When we meditate upon Scripture, God reveals his relationship to us, our relationship to him, and our relationship to others.

In *Think it,* I see, I hear, I feel, I smell, I taste, and I am here.

Doing the Discipline: Lectio Divina

Practice the spiritual discipline of meditation via *lectio divina*.

Request to Be in His Presence

"Dear Lord, bring me into the context of Your world."

1. ***Read it***—select a portion, a phrase within the reading.
2. ***Think it***—mull it over in your mind, thinking about the context and setting, reimagining the event, putting yourself into the situation. As you meditate, use all five senses to re-create the context and the setting by building upon the images that are supplied within the passages. For example, select "*I urge you, brothers, in view of God's mercy, to offer your bodies as living sacrifices.*" Now, imagine yourself standing with other believers in someone's home early one Sunday morning (what do you suppose it may have looked like, smelled like, sounded like?), hearing someone recite a letter that was just received from the apostle Paul as he awaits his trial before Caesar's court in Rome and very likely his own execution. How might the reader have recited "I urge you, brothers, in view of God's mercy, to offer your bodies as living sacrifices."? How might the crowd have reacted when they heard it? What questions do you imagine rang out? And, from whom? What is my reaction? What do I make of what was just said?

List what you see, hear, feel, smell, and taste, things that caught your attention, that perhaps, you hadn't noticed before.

- we must die to Self
  to self seeking desires

Give Thanks to the Lord

"Thank You, Lord, for what You are doing in me and for what You want to accomplish in this world through me."

Prayer

Pray for each member of your community.

Redrawing Your Brain Map

DAY FOUR

Prayer

Dear Lord, today give me opportunity to show my faith by my actions. I realize that I must retrain myself to believe what You believe. Help me to engage in the disciplines that are necessary for me to displace my erroneous beliefs and are crucial to fully incorporate Your beliefs into my mind. Amen.

Core Thought

Change is rejecting a common false belief.

The American church has taught that *faith is agreement* with religious doctrines. This has led people to think they are disciples by simply agreeing with the concepts presented by Christ (i.e., believing them to be true) and then receiving the benefits of eternal life and relief from the guilt of sin. This has led to a weak church populated by members who think they have believed, when in fact they have not. They have not believed because *biblical faith entails following, and following is an action.* Simply stated biblical faith, believing in Christ, and trusting Jesus is not present where action is absent. One cannot properly claim to believe in Jesus and at the same time not trust what He has said, such as that He is Lord over all, and what He commanded anyone who would be His disciple to do, for example obeying His commands.

Today's Exercises

Core Scripture: Romans 12:1-2

Read aloud Romans 12:1-2.

Recite this week's memory verses aloud five times.

> Therefore, I urge you, brothers, in view of God's mercy, to offer your bodies as living sacrifices, holy and pleasing to God—this is your spiritual act of worship. Do not conform any longer to the pattern of this world, but be transformed by the renewing of your mind. Then you will be able to test and approve what God's will is—his good, pleasing and perfect will.

Discovering the Discipline: Lectio Divina

Oratio – Pray it

Today, we will learn and practice the third element in RSR, *Pray it.* Here we pray the text. When we move from *Think it* to *Pray it,* we move from exploration to examination. In *Think it*, the world of the Scriptures entered into us, and we began to explore it. In *Pray it*, we move within the world of the Scriptures and they begin to examine us. When we pray the Scriptures we are searching and being searched. "Bible searching and searching prayer go hand in hand. What we receive from God in the Book's message we return to Him with interest in prayer."[5] Peterson writes, "Spiritual reading requires a disciplined attention to exactly the way the text is written; it requires a meditative and receptive entering into the world of the text; and it requires response."[6] The response is made by prayer: "the Scriptures, read and prayed, are our primary and normative access to God as he reveals himself to us. . . . Prayer detached from Scripture, from listening to God, disconnected from God's words to us, short-circuits the relational language that is prayer. . . . Prayer is access to everything that God is for us: holiness, justice, mercy, forgiveness, sovereignty, blessing,

5. P.T. Forsythe quoted in Peterson, *Eat This Book,* 103.

6. Peterson.

vindication, salvation, love, majesty, glory. . . . Prayer brings us into the welcoming presence of God as he generously offers himself, just as he is, to us."[7] It is as we pray the Scriptures that God reveals His will to us.

In *Pray it*, God's Spirit tells us what it is about ourselves that must be renewed. He also tells us what part we are responsible for carrying out in His mission to reconcile all things to Himself. *Pray it* is the conversation we have with God, where He speaks with us about what is true about our relationship with Him, what must be done to strengthen it, and our relation to others and what we must do to bring about its restoration.

It is in *Pray it* that we accept the truth that God is telling us and our responsibility to do what is necessary to change those things about us that are keeping us from accomplishing His will, through our lives.

In *Pray it,* I understand, I accept, I admit it, and I will do with Your power and direction what You require to make the changes in my life that must be done.

Doing the Discipline: Lectio Divina

Practice the spiritual discipline of meditation via *lectio divina*.

Request to Be in His Presence

"Dear Lord, bring me into the context of Your world."

1. ***Read it***
2. ***Think it***
3. ***Pray it***—today, using the list you made yesterday in *Think it*, ask God to give you understanding into how the truths He has spoken in these Scriptures apply to you now. Ask, "What is it about me that I need to deal with? What is it about me that must change?"

---

7. Peterson, 104.

Respond to God by accepting and admitting whatever responsibility is implied by what He has shown.

Write what it is that God has shown you, and what you must admit responsibility for having done (or not done).

Give Thanks to the Lord

"Thank You, Lord, for what You are doing in me and for what You want to accomplish in this world through me."

Prayer

Pray for each member of your community.

Redrawing Your Brain Map

DAY FIVE

Prayer

Dear Lord, help me to know the things that need to change about me. Be gentle with me when You are revealing the values that I have accepted as being true but which are incompatible with being a devoted disciple of Jesus. Help me to identify the actions that I have turned into habits and must cease. And help me to replace these with habits that will transform me into someone who will love doing what You love done. Help me to know *what needs to grow* and *what needs to go*. Amen.

Core Thought

Change is acquiring the common true beliefs.

Yesterday, we saw that a faith which claims to believe in Jesus but lacks the actions associated with following Jesus is a contradiction in terms. It is crucial that we purge from our minds any of that modern notion of faith and recover the biblical notion of faith.

The issue before us then is how to redraw our mental maps to recover biblical faith, *faith as following,* and then rethink what it means to be a Christian. Getting out of our minds the deeply rutted groove of a forgiveness-only gospel and replacing it with the gospel that Jesus believes takes time. It requires deprogramming and reprogramming the mind, which the apostle Paul admonishes: "Do not conform any longer to the pattern of this world, but be transformed by the renewing of your mind" (Romans 12:2). Paul prefaces his command by explaining that engaging in the process of renewing our mind is a sacrificial act, an act of worshipping God, "Therefore, I urge you, brothers, in view of God's mercy, to offer your bodies as living sacrifices, holy and pleasing to God — this is your spiritual act of worship" (Romans 12:1).

For Paul, engaging in the disciplines that bring about our spiritual transformation is worship, the expression of our love for God in action. It is by this renewal process that the Spirit of God transform us.

Today's Exercises

Core Scripture: Romans 12:1-2

Read aloud Romans 12:1-2.

Recite this week's memory verses aloud five times.

> Therefore, I urge you, brothers, in view of God's mercy, to offer your bodies as living sacrifices, holy and pleasing to God — this is your spiritual act of worship. Do not conform any longer to the pattern of this world, but be transformed by the renewing of your mind. Then you will be able to test and approve what God's will is — his good, pleasing and perfect will.

Discovering the Discipline: Lectio Divina

Live It

Today, we will learn and practice the fourth and final element in LD, *Live it*. Here we live the text.

From *Read it* to *Think it*, we move from the words in the Scripture into the presence of God's Word (Jesus) present within the Scriptures. When we move from *Think it* to *Pray it*, we move from a personal exploration of God's Word to being personally examined and revealed by the illuminating power of God's Word. This revealing by God causes us to respond in two ways. First, in *Pray it* we respond to what God reveals to us in the language of prayer; this we might call spiritual-language. Secondly, in *Live it*, we respond to God in the language of action; this we might call body language.

In *Live it,* we take all that God has said in *Read it,* and all we have seen in *Think it*, and all that we declare that we will do in *Pray it*, and offer it to God in acts of worship. *Live it* is the offering of our bodies to

God the Father as living sacrifices in acts of worship.[8]

To offer our bodies to God means to give to God what our bodies do for us. Our bodies act for us. They do what our wills direct them to do. So to offer our body to God is to give Him our body to act-out or live-out what His will directs. In *Live it*, I live the text. I do it before Him, and I do it for Him.

Doing the Discipline: Lectio Divina

Practice the spiritual discipline of meditation via *lectio divina*.

Request to Be in His Presence

"Dear Lord, bring me into the context of Your world."

1. ***Read it***
2. ***Think it***
3. ***Pray it***
4. ***Live it***—first, review what you wrote down yesterday, what you admitted responsibility for having done (or not done). Next, ask God to reveal to you what He wants you to do about what you have admitted.

Now, list what particular action(s) you will take today to accomplish what God has revealed for you to do.

---

8. Our modern narrow notion of contemplation misleads us into thinking that to contemplate means to do something within one's mind, as opposed to doing something with one's body. The modern notion insists that what is being done is only occurring between our head's temples. The proper notion has to do with where one's body is making an offering to God (i.e., before God in the *templum*) where offerings to God are to be received. For Christians, we offer our bodies to God in acts of service to others (Matthew 25:34-40, Romans 12:2).

Lastly, pray asking the Holy Spirit to empower you to act in obedience, and to accomplish what He has revealed for you to do today.

Give Thanks to the Lord

"Thank You, Lord, for what You are doing in me and for what You want to accomplish in this world through me."

Prayer

Pray for each member of your community.

Redrawing Your Brain Map

DAY SIX

Community Meeting

In preparation for this week's meeting, you will have read and reflected upon each of the week's five Core Thoughts, recorded your thoughts and observations, and are ready to recite this week's memory verses to the group.

WEEK 2

Recovering Biblical Faith

DAY ONE

Prayer

Dear Lord, teach me what it is to be faithful. I suspect that I may have a somewhat defective idea of what it is to have faith. I want to know what true faith is. I want to believe as You believed. I want my life to be pleasing in Your sight, joyful for me, and healing for all that come in contact with You, through me. Amen.

Core Thought

Faith is perfected by obedience.

In the earliest letter of the New Testament, penned by the leader of the first church in Jerusalem, James explained the difference between the way Jesus believed what He believed (i.e., biblical faith), and the kind of faith some of his church members were demonstrating:

> What good is it, dear brothers and sisters, if you say you have faith but don't show it by your actions? Can that kind of faith save anyone? . . . So you see, faith by itself isn't enough. Unless it produces good deeds, it is dead and useless. (James 2:14,17, NLT).

Another way to say this is that a person who claims to have true, biblical faith and yet is not consistently seen doing good deeds does not have the real, life-changing biblical faith at all. What James is arguing is that this so-called faith which this person is believing is useless because nothing results from its being believed or not believed. If this person's faith doesn't change anything (either himself or anyone else), then it is like a dead thing, which can do nothing. If this faith does nothing, then it is useless. This is James's way of saying that having this kind of faith, a faith that actually changes nothing, is not biblical faith.

To say that faith is only real in obedience is to mean that to have true faith one must believe as Jesus believed. From this faith comes "the victory that overcomes the world."

Today's Exercises

Core Scripture: James 2:14-26

Read aloud James 2:14-26.

Recite this week's memory verses aloud five times.

> As the body without the spirit is dead, so faith without deeds is dead. (James 2:26)

Doing the Discipline: Lectio Divina

Practice the spiritual discipline of meditation via *lectio divina*. This week, practice using all four elements, *Read it, Think it, Pray it*, and *Live it*, each day. Remember to select only a small portion of each day's reading upon which to meditate. Trying to meditate upon too large a portion of Scripture is as difficult and unrewarding as is trying to slowly enjoy the flavor of a well prepared piece of meat while you are choking. As you practice LD you may find it difficult to complete all the steps during one day's session. Don't fret, just mark where you left off and continue from that point on during your next session. What should you do when it seems like it "isn't working"? Remember, when you are doing LD you are offering this time as a gift (a sacrifice) to the Lord. It is His to do with as He desires. You have offered this time to Him during which you are making yourself available to be present with Him. You are ready to listen and learn if that's what He has in mind. Because LD is a gift from you to Him, to use as He wants with no strings attached, it will never fail!

Request to Be in His Presence

"Dear Lord, bring me into the context of Your world."

1. ***Read it***—read James 2:14-17 at least twice, preferably out loud.

   What good is it, my brothers, if a man claims to have faith but has no deeds? Can such a faith save him? Suppose a brother or sister is without clothes and daily food. If one of you says to him, "Go, I wish you well; keep warm and well fed," but does nothing about his physical needs, what good is it? In the same way, faith by itself, if it is not accompanied by action, is dead.

2. ***Think it***—select a portion, a phrase within the reading (for example, select *"Suppose a brother or sister is without clothes and daily food. If one of you says to him, "Go, I wish you well; keep warm and well fed," but does nothing about his physical needs, what good is it?").* Mull it over in your mind, thinking about the context and setting, reimagining the event, putting yourself into the situation. As you meditate, use all five senses to re-create the context and the setting by building upon the images that are supplied within the passages.

   List what you see, hear, feel, smell, and taste, things that caught your attention, that perhaps, you hadn't noticed before.

3. ***Pray it***—ask God to give you understanding into how the truths He has spoken in these Scriptures apply to you now. Ask, "What is it about me that I need to deal with? What is it about me that must change?"

Respond to God by accepting and admitting whatever responsibility is implied by what He has shown.

I have a Responsibility to Be God's hands, feet, voice, and difference maker to those in need.

Write what it is that God has shown you, and what you must admit responsibility for having done (or not done).

I have not been very caring to those who walk into our Church looking for money.
They may have a real need

4. ***Live it***—ask God to reveal to you what He wants you to do about what you have admitted.

List what particular action(s) you will take today to accomplish what God has revealed for you to do.

Give Thanks to the Lord

"Thank You, Lord, for what You are doing in me and for what You want to accomplish in this world through me."

Prayer

Pray for each member of your community.

Recovering Biblical Faith

DAY TWO

Prayer

Dear Lord, it is easy for me to *agree* with what Jesus says in the Bible. It is just as easy to *agree* with what my minister teaches each Sunday at church. What is hard for me is *doing* what Jesus commands. I know that You want me to show my love for You by doing what You've told me to do. Lord, train me to be obedient to the things that you command. Amen.

Core Thought

Faith is performed by hearing and obeying.

It was often the case that when Jesus would teach a large crowd that had gathered before Him, He would do so using a parable after which He would finish by saying "he who has ears to hear, let him hear." By this, Jesus taught the disciples that there are two kinds of people who hear what it is that He says.

The first kind of hearers are the kind that hear the words, see the point, and maybe even agree with what Jesus has taught, but that is as far as Jesus' words will affect them because their "heart [is] calloused; they hardly hear . . . and they . . . closed their eyes" (Matthew 13:15). The second kind of hearers hear Jesus' words and agree. They "understand with their hearts," and His words move them to respond by doing what He has said: They "are blessed and turn," and then they are healed.

Jesus taught His disciples that authentic faith is present only in those who have taken Jesus' word to heart. They have truly believed *what* Jesus has said to be true *because* they believe *in* Jesus, and they truly believe His words are true about them. They "understand with the heart." This kind of understanding causes them to act in obedience so that they turn or repent. Those with authentic faith respond to Jesus' words by obeying.

Today's Exercises

Core Scripture: James 2:14-26

Read aloud James 2:14-26.

Recite this week's memory verses aloud five times.

> As the body without the spirit is dead, so faith without deeds is dead. (James 2:26)

Doing the Discipline: Lectio Divina

Practice the spiritual discipline of meditation via *lectio divina.*

Request to Be in His Presence

"Dear Lord, bring me into the context of Your world."

1. ***Read it***—read James 2:18-19 at least twice, preferably out loud.

   But someone will say, "You have ***faith***; I have ***deeds***."

   Show me your ***faith*** without ***deeds***, and I will show you my ***faith*** by what I ***do***. You ***believe*** that there is one God. Good! Even the demons ***believe*** that and ***shudder***. (emphasis added)

2. ***Think it***—select a portion, a phrase within the reading (for example, select *"You believe that there is one God. Good! Even the demons believe that and shudder").* Mull it over in your mind, thinking about the context and setting, reimagining the event, putting yourself into the situation. As you meditate, use all five senses to re-create the context and the setting by building upon the images that are supplied within the passages.

List what you see, hear, feel, smell, and taste.

vv18-19 Meditated on

Our Head Knowledge must be embraced by our Heart for Faith to be of value to us.

3. ***Pray it***—ask God to give you insight into the situation and also your life. Ask, "What is it about me that I need to deal with? What is it about me that must change?"

   Respond to what God is revealing to you by asking Him what He wants you to understand.

   When you understand, respond to God by accepting and admitting whatever responsibility is implied by His revelation. State what it is that God has revealed that you must admit responsibility for doing.

4. ***Live it***—ask God to empower you to act in obedience, and to accomplish what He has revealed for you to do today.

   State what particular action(s) you will take today to accomplish what God has revealed for you to do.

Give Thanks to the Lord

"Thank You, Lord, for what You are doing in me and for what You want to accomplish in this world through me."

Prayer

Pray for each member of your community.

Recovering Biblical Faith

DAY THREE

Prayer

Dear Lord, sometimes it seems like I must not love You enough to do as You say. Please train me to love You by being obedient. Help me to change from being one who is satisfied with merely agreeing to one who enjoys performing for You. Train me in such a way that when I feel my obedience is getting me nowhere, I will continue to perform for You, if for no other reason than that I know that my obedience gives You pleasure. Amen.

Core Thought

Faith is persistence in prayer.

Jesus uses the *Parable of the Persistent Widow* to teach His disciples that "they should always pray and not give up" (Luke 18:1-8). In teaching the parable, Jesus uses a common rabbinical teaching tool to convey His message called "How much more." This method is sometimes named when it is used, as where Jesus says, "If you then, though you are evil, know how to give good gifts to your children, *how much more* will your Father in heaven give the Holy Spirit to those who ask him!" (Luke 11:13, emphasis added). In our parable it is not mentioned but is implied by how Jesus presents His argument. His argument goes as follows:

> If you are as persistent in your praying to God (as was the widow who kept coming and bothering the uncaring, unconcerned, unjust judge, who eventually gave her what she requested), then, how much more will God, the most caring,

> most concerned, and most just judge, give you, soon, what you ask of Him?

The parable teaches that if you are persistent in your praying to God then God will give you, soon, what you ask Him for. Jesus then adds the phrase "when the Son of Man comes, will he find *faith* [as seen in the persistence of the widow in the parable] on the earth?" (Luke 18:8, emphasis added).

By identifying faith as the widow's persistent action as the example of what He expects His followers to be found *doing* when He returns, Jesus teaches that authentic faith is found only in those whose faith is seen in the persistent, continuing action of praying.

Today's Exercises

Core Scripture: James 2:14-26

Read aloud James 2:14-26.

Recite this week's memory verse aloud five times.

> As the body without the spirit is dead, so faith without deeds is dead. (James 2:26)

Doing the Discipline: Lectio Divina

Practice the spiritual discipline of meditation via *lectio divina*.

Request to Be in His Presence

"Dear Lord, bring me into the context of Your world."

1. ***Read it***—read James 2:20-22 at least twice, preferably out loud.

> You foolish man, do you want evidence that *faith without deeds* is *useless*? Was not our ancestor *Abraham considered righteous* for what *he did* when he offered his son Isaac on the altar? You see that *his faith* and *his actions* were *working together*, and *his faith* was *made complete* by what *he did*. (emphasis added)

2. ***Think it***—select a portion, a phrase within the reading (for example, select *"You see that his faith and his actions were working together, and his faith was made complete by what he did.")*. Mull it over in your mind, thinking about the context and setting, reimagining the event, putting yourself into the situation. As you meditate, use all five senses to re-create the context and the setting by building upon the images that are supplied within the passages.

   List what you see, hear, feel, smell, and taste.

3. ***Pray it***—ask God to give you insight into the situation and also your life. Ask, "What is it about me that I need to deal with? What is it about me that must change?"

   Respond to what God is revealing to you by asking Him what He wants you to understand.

   When you understand, respond to God by accepting and admitting whatever responsibility is implied by His revelation. State what it is that God has revealed that you must admit responsibility for doing.

4. ***Live it***—ask God to empower you to act in obedience, and to accomplish what He has revealed for you to do today.

   State what particular action(s) you will take today to accomplish what God has revealed for you to do.

Give Thanks to the Lord

"Thank You, Lord, for what You are doing in me and for what You want to accomplish in this world through me."

Prayer

Pray for each member of your community.

Recovering Biblical Faith

DAY FOUR

Prayer

Dear Lord, train me to be concerned about accomplishing whatever it is that You wish me to do. I am inclined to consider first of all what's in it for me. Begin to show me this day how to be delighted in fulfilling Your agenda. Amen.

Core Thought

> Faith is patiently following where Jesus leads.

The disciples began to follow Jesus because they believed that He was the Messiah. They believed that when the Messiah appeared on the scene, He would *immediately* overthrow the current government, the people would proclaim Him king of all the lands, and He would rule as the new Jewish king. So with this understanding they followed Jesus, thinking Jesus was calling them to be the new leaders over all the people. They thought that Jesus' calling was preparing them to begin ruling in glory *now.* Instead, He was preparing them to die like Him on their crosses now and rule with Him in glory later. The disciples' immediate agenda did not match Jesus' agenda.

Jesus corrected the disciples' thinking as to how they were to fulfill His calling and where He was leading. "If anyone would come after me, he must deny himself and take up his cross daily and follow me" (Luke 9:23).

In short, Jesus expects His followers to follow Him.

To follow Jesus, one must "deny himself." This means that we must abandon our own agenda for our lives. It means that we must not obey the inner voice of our own desires, which are conformed to the pattern of this world. In order to stop this voice from asserting its rule over us, we are to "take up our cross daily."

We are to begin a daily routine of crucifying ourselves, causing that inner voice to die in silence. Along with this routine of killing that inner voice, Jesus says "follow me," commanding us to live His life. As we live this life, that inner voice is silenced and is replaced by a renewed inner voice which begins to lead us.

As we continue to take up our cross and follow Jesus, that voice becomes easier to recognize. It is the voice of the Good Shepherd as He gently leads His flock.

Today's Exercises

Core Scripture: James 2:14-16
Read aloud James 2:14-26.
Recite this week's memory verse aloud five times.

> As the body without the spirit is dead, so faith without deeds is dead. (James 2:26)

Doing the Discipline: Lectio Divina

Practice the spiritual discipline of meditation via *lectio divina*.

Request to Be in His Presence

"Dear Lord, bring me into the context of Your world."

1. ***Read it***—read James 2:23-24 at least twice, preferably out loud.

> And the scripture was fulfilled that says, "Abraham *believed* God, and it was *credited to him as righteousness*," and he was called God's friend. You see that a person is *justified by what he does* and not by faith alone. (emphasis added)

2. ***Think it***—select a portion, a phrase within the reading (for example, select *"Abraham believed God, and it was credited to him as righteousness," and he was called God's friend).* Mull it over in your mind, thinking about the context and setting, reimagining the event, putting yourself into the situation. As you meditate, use all five senses to re-create the context and the setting by building upon the images that are supplied within the passages.

   List what you see, hear, feel, smell, and taste.

3. ***Pray it***—ask God to give you insight into the situation and also your life. Ask, "What is it about me that I need to deal with? What is it about me that must change?"

   Respond to what God is revealing to you by asking Him what He wants you to understand.

   When you understand, respond to God by accepting and admitting whatever responsibility is implied by His revelation. State what it is that God has revealed that you must admit responsibility for doing.

4. ***Live it***—ask God to empower you to act in obedience, and to accomplish what He has revealed for you to do today.

   State what particular action(s) you will take today to accomplish what God has revealed for you to do.

Give Thanks to the Lord

"Thank You, Lord, for what You are doing in me and for what You want to accomplish in this world through me."

Prayer

Pray for each member of your community.

Recovering Biblical Faith

DAY FIVE

Prayer

Dear Lord, I realize that if I really did believe that obeying You was the most important and urgent thing for me to do, then I would find it hard to proceed as if it wasn't. I believe I do have a trust problem. Please help me to train in ways that will build up in me the assurance that comes from trusting in You. Amen.

Core Thought

Faith is proceeding with confidence.

When Scripture speaks of faith, it almost always does so by giving examples showing believers being obedient to what God had commanded them to do. Often the examples show their continued obedience despite what appears to them to be the very reason why they should not proceed. What caused them to proceed with confidence when common sense and all the usual signs and the facts of the matter and given the normal course of events they should have retreated? The author of Hebrews says it was their *faith*, their confident assurance:

> What is faith? It is the confident assurance that what we hope for is going to happen. It is the evidence of things we cannot yet see . . . It is impossible to please God without faith. Anyone who wants to come to him must believe that there is a God and that he rewards those who sincerely seek him. (Hebrews 11:1, 6, NLT, 1996)

Faith provides us the assurance we need to proceed confidently because we have learned that we can trust ourselves to God's care. To put it simply, faith is proceeding based on trusting.

The principle that faith, rooted in trust, will always lead to action is fundamental to the Scripture. That is why we can hardly talk about faith without having to resort to examples of believers acting it out. It is because we are sure that we can trust Jesus that our faith proceeds confidently from us in our actions. Faith is proceeding with confidence, based upon truly believing what Jesus believed—that God the Father surely is worthy of our trust.

Today's Exercises
Core Scripture: James 2:14-26
Read aloud James 2:14-26.
Recite this week's memory verse aloud five times.

> As the body without the spirit is dead, so faith without deeds is dead (James 2:26).

Doing the Discipline: Lectio Divina
Practice the spiritual discipline of meditation via *lectio divina*.

Request to Be in His Presence
"Dear Lord, bring me into the context of Your world."

1. ***Read it***—read James 2:25-26 at least twice, preferably out loud.

> In the same way, was not even Rahab the prostitute *considered righteous* for what she did when she gave lodging to the spies and sent them off in a different direction? As the *body* without the *spirit* is dead, so *faith* without *deeds* is dead. (emphasis added)

2. ***Think it***—select a portion, a phrase within the reading (for example, select *"As the body without the spirit is dead, so faith without deeds is dead").* Mull it over in your mind, thinking about the context and setting, reimagining the event, putting yourself into the situation. As you meditate, use all five senses to re-create the context and the setting by building upon the images that are supplied within the passages.

   List what you see, hear, feel, smell, and taste.

3. ***Pray it***—ask God to give you insight into the situation and also your life. Ask, "What is it about me that I need to deal with? What is it about me that must change?"

   Respond to what God is revealing to you by asking Him what He wants you to understand.

   When you understand, respond to God by accepting and admitting whatever responsibility is implied by His revelation. State what it is that God has revealed that you must admit responsibility for doing.

4. ***Live it***—ask God to empower you to act in obedience, and to accomplish what He has revealed for you to do today.

   State what particular action(s) you will take today to accomplish what God has revealed for you to do.

Give Thanks to the Lord

"Thank You, Lord, for what You are doing in me and for what You want to accomplish in this world through me."

Prayer

Pray for each member of your community.

Recovering Biblical Faith

DAY SIX

Community Meeting

In preparation for this week's meeting, you will have read and reflected upon each of the week's five Core Thoughts, recorded your thoughts and observations, and are ready to recite this week's memory verses to the group.

WEEK 3

Rebuilding the Gospel from the Ground Up

DAY ONE

Prayer

Dear Lord, this week I want to open my mind to be able to explore what the gospel is. Help me to test what I hear by the simpler truths You have already revealed to me in Your Word. Help me not to reject an idea that is new to me simply on that basis alone. Give me wisdom and a discerning mind. Amen.

Core Thought

The gospel of consumer Christianity is no gospel at all.

We live in a world where two ways or philosophies are at war. The first philosophy is the Jesus way, the way of self-sacrifice, submission, humility, and patience. It is the worldview of Jesus with God at its center and where His disciples live for others, because Jesus was a man for others. In the Jesus way, it is not about us. It is about God. The Jesus way shows us that the means are just as important as the ends.

The other philosophy, which dominates, is the consumer culture. It is a world of consumption, assertiveness, speed, and fame. In the consumer world it is all about me. In the Jesus way, Jesus becomes more. In the consumer culture, man becomes more.

The consumer culture creates the consumer church, which produces consumer Christians. In this consumer Christian culture, the gospel is about receiving benefits and getting into heaven. The message is about man rather than God. It is about the cultivation of artificial needs, an environment of instant gratification, the teaching of Scripture in neat formulas, and worship centered on fulfilling personal needs according to individual taste.

These worlds are at war; they are mortal enemies. The alarming thing is that many good Christian people live without ever knowing they have been seduced by culture. They are unaware that the consumer Christianity's priorities and practices work against forming Christ's character in them and instead result in creating more and better religious consumers, "nice," "moral" people whose life and religion matters little to others, and ultimately leaves them unsatisfied.

This week we will explore the Jesus way, contrasting it with its enemy, the current culture of consumer Christianity. We will obey Paul's command to reject the different gospel and rebuild the True Gospel from the ground up (Galatians 1:1-12).

Today's Exercises

Core Scripture: Mark 8:27-38

Read aloud Mark 8:27-38.

Recite this week's memory verses aloud five times.

> If anyone would come after me, he must deny himself and take up his cross and follow me. For whoever wants to save his life will lose it, but whoever loses his life for me and for the gospel will save it (Mark 8:34-35).

Doing the Discipline: Lectio Divina

Practice the spiritual discipline of meditation via *lectio divina*.

Request to Be in His Presence

"Dear Lord, bring me into the context of Your world."

1. ***Read it***—read Mark 8:27-30 at least twice, preferably out loud.
2. ***Think it***—mull it over in your mind, thinking about the context and setting, reimagining the event, putting yourself into the

situation. As you meditate, use all five senses to re-create the context and the setting by building the images that are supplied within the passages.

List what you see, hear, feel, smell, and taste.

3. ***Pray it***—ask God to give you insight into the situation and also your life. Ask, "What is it about me that I need to deal with? What is it about me that must change?"

   Respond to what God is revealing to you by asking Him what He wants you to understand.

   When you understand, respond to God by accepting and admitting whatever responsibility is implied by His revelation. State what it is that God has revealed that you must admit responsibility for doing.

4. ***Live it***—ask God to empower you to act in obedience, and to accomplish what He has revealed for you to do today.

   State what particular action(s) you will take today to accomplish what God has revealed for you to do.

Give Thanks to the Lord

"Thank You, Lord, for what You are doing in me and for what You want to accomplish in this world through me."

Journal

Record ideas, impressions, feelings, questions, and any insights you may have had during your time of meditation.

Prayer

Pray for each member of your community.

Rebuilding the Gospel from the Ground Up

DAY TWO

Prayer

Dear Lord, I want not just to know about You. Help me to believe in You. Teach me that I can believe in You and trust You. Amen.

Core Thought

The gospel places prayer before competence.

Jesus modeled prayer as a priority. His actions demonstrated that His relationship with His Father was the basis for ministry. He prayed all night before important decisions and slipped away to spend time with his Father. He sought to relish His relationship with His Father and in turn could answer the priority question, the only question that really counts: What is the will of God?

Theologian Dietrich Bonhoeffer left Germany in 1939 for New York City to teach at Union Theological Seminary. His friends and mentors thought it was wise to spare him the Nazi persecution of the church. He would be able to return to teach and rebuild Germany after the war. Bonhoeffer sought God's wisdom and he believed that there was only one important question: What is the will of God? He took the last ship back to Germany before World War II began. He was executed in 1939 for his part in a conspiracy to kill Hitler. It is the antithesis of consumer Christianity to take an action which is sacrificial.

The consumer way is to act now, make an impact, get things done. The great temptation of the consumer way is to lead with competence. The myth of competence is twofold.

The first is that after a period of time in the Christian way, we know enough and have cleaned up our life enough that we can get by without practicing disciplines such as prayer, solitude, meditation—the kinds of actions that build our dependence on God. The disciplines require us to take repeated actions over and over again. The culmination of repeated action is habit, which creates character.

The myth is that we have some control over the nastier parts of our nature. We feel safe and secure in our own ability to function. We are over the really bad stuff.

The second part of the myth of competence is that we can get the job done without contemplation. In the end, consumer Christianity, which depends on personal competence rather than a prayerful life of dependence on God proves not to be a way at all. It is only a disappointing cul-de-sac. The Jesus way is a life of prayer, silence, solitude, and meditation, which multiplies and enhances one's competence. The Jesus way is the Way of Truth and Light.

Today's Exercises

Core Scripture: Mark 8:27-38

Read aloud Mark 8:27-38.

Recite this week's memory verses aloud five times.

> If anyone would come after me, he must deny himself and take up his cross and follow me. For whoever wants to save his life will lose it, but whoever loses his life for me and for the gospel will save it (Mark 8:34-35).

Doing the Discipline: Lectio Divina

Practice the spiritual discipline of meditation via *lectio divina.*

Request to Be in His Presence

"Dear Lord, bring me into the context of Your world."

1. ***Read it***—read Mark 8:31-33 at least twice, preferably out loud.
2. ***Think it***—mull it over in your mind, thinking about the context

and setting, reimagining the event, putting yourself into the situation. As you meditate, use all five senses to re-create the context and the setting by building the images that are supplied within the passages.

List what you see, hear, feel, smell, and taste.

3. ***Pray it***—ask God to give you insight into the situation and also your life. Ask, "What is it about me that I need to deal with? What is it about me that must change?"

   Respond to what God is revealing to you by asking Him what He wants you to understand.

   I wrestle with Phrase "Get behind me Satan"

   When you understand, respond to God by accepting and admitting whatever responsibility is implied by His revelation. State what it is that God has revealed that you must admit responsibility for doing.

   - lay down life - Sacrifice
   - Take up cross? Accept God's path for your life
   - Follow Me - obey + follow His leading

4. ***Live it***—ask God to empower you to act in obedience, and to accomplish what He has revealed for you to do today.

   State what particular action(s) you will take today to accomplish what God has revealed for you to do.

Give Thanks to the Lord

"Thank You, Lord, for what You are doing in me and for what You want to accomplish in this world through me."

Journal

Record ideas, impressions, feelings, questions, and any insights you may have had during your time of meditation.

Prayer

Pray for each member of your community.

Rebuilding the Gospel from the Ground Up

DAY THREE

Prayer

Dear Lord, help me to transform my desire to have things that bring me pleasure, which I think will satisfy my wanting, into being satisfied by doing the things that You desire and to enjoy the pleasure it gives You. Amen.

Core Thought

The gospel values community above individualism.

Ever since the Renaissance, a revival in art and literature, and the Enlightenment, a philosophical movement based on rationalism and skepticism, God has been moved out of the center and replaced by man. This human-centered worldview taught that individual rights, individual thoughts, and individual needs are paramount. This was a serious shift from the previous worldview that valued community and, in religious terms, the congregation.

The congregation is the local home base where the Christian life is formed. It is where our identity is developed. The congregation is not about us—it is about God. God's plan is to create a new community where His disciples learn to love Him by loving one another. The operating biblical metaphor for worship is sacrifice. We gather to contribute to one another's lives. We come to the altar to sacrifice, serve, and set aside our personal agenda. We, like Jesus, then choose to live the life of submission to others, to put their needs equal to ours and even more important than our own.

Individualism uses the congregation and turns it into a consumer enterprise. We live in a culture that is dependent upon wanting and acquiring more. The advertising industry stirs up needs in us that we didn't know we had. Christian leaders have joined in with gusto. We have recast the gospel into consumer items, entertainment, adventure, problem solving, and formulas to help us get an edge. We have learned that the way to get a crowd is to offer them what the society teaches them they need. We have become world-class consumers of religious goods and services.

The present system of discipleship offered in a consumer package targeted at individual needs is not sufficient to form people into the image of Christ. Study without reflection, measuring maturity by knowledge, and finishing curriculum has no traction. This is not the way Jesus brings conformity to His will. The consumer Christian culture makes us become more and Jesus becomes less. This is not the way our sacrificial lives become available to others. This is the antithesis of the sacrificial, deny-yourself servant that Jesus was and has called us to be.

Today's Exercises

Core Scripture: Mark 8:27-38

Read aloud Mark 8:27-38.

Recite this week's memory verses aloud five times.

> If anyone would come after me, he must deny himself and take up his cross and follow me. For whoever wants to save his life will lose it, but whoever loses his life for me and for the gospel will save it (Mark 8:34-35).

Doing the Discipline: Lectio Divina

Practice the spiritual discipline of meditation via *lectio divina*.

Request to Be in His Presence

"Dear Lord, bring me into the context of Your world."

1. ***Read it***—read Mark 8:34-35 at least twice, preferably out loud.
2. ***Think it***—mull it over in your mind, thinking about the context and setting, reimagining the event, putting yourself into the situation. As you meditate, use all five senses to re-create the context and the setting by building the images that are supplied within the passages.

   List what you see, hear, feel, smell, and taste.

3. ***Pray it***—ask God to give you insight into the situation and also your life. Ask, "What is it about me that I need to deal with? What is it about me that must change?"

   Respond to what God is revealing to you by asking Him what He wants you to understand.

   When you understand, respond to God by accepting and admitting whatever responsibility is implied by His revelation. State what it is that God has revealed that you must admit responsibility for doing.

4. ***Live it***—ask God to empower you to act in obedience, and to accomplish what He has revealed for you to do today.

   State what particular action(s) you will take today to accomplish what God has revealed for you to do.

Give Thanks to the Lord

"Thank You, Lord, for what You are doing in me and for what You want to accomplish in this world through me."

Journal

Record ideas, impressions, feelings, questions, and any insights you may have had during your time of meditation.

Prayer

Pray for each member of your community.

Rebuilding the Gospel from the Ground Up

DAY FOUR

Prayer

Dear Lord, train me to be someone who brings refreshment into the lives of the people I come in contact with today. Let me be Your presence to them, bring restoration in their lives. Help me to reveal You, today. Amen.

Core Thought

The gospel values patient endurance above impatient accomplishment.

Impatience is the most accepted sin in America. We are an impetuous people. Everything seems to be available now, and we have been trained to expect it now. The Internet appeases our insatiable appetite for instant knowledge and for goods and services in minutes. The culture is getting faster, and the faster we move, the less we become. Today's church attendees want relief and answers today and if not today, at the latest, tomorrow. This culture wants leaders who service them, not those who will challenge and change them. But this "spiritual fast food" will destroy us.

In the film *Super Size Me*, a young man gains thirty pounds and develops associated problems eating three meals a day for thirty days at McDonald's.[1] When we read the Bible to fulfill our potential, get a handle on principles, get the edge on others, or increase our capacity at work, we turn the life-giving Word into more of the same terminal

1. *Super Size Me: A Film of Epic Portions* DVD, Morgan Spurlock (directed by Samuel Goldwyn Films, 2004).

fast food. If treating the Word of God like fast food worked, then why, when we are stuffed so full of knowledge, do we live so badly?

Don't read the Bible to enhance your self-image. Read it to receive, respond, submit, and listen to God's voice so we can serve and humbly obey. Read under the authority of God's Word, not to get ahead. Karl Barth said, "I have read many books, but the Bible reads me." As Jesus said, "Everyone who hears these words of mine and puts them into practice is like a wise man who built his house on the rock" (Matthew 7:24).

The formation of character into the person of Christ can't be hurried. It's a slow work, and it gets very messy. People fail, delay, make mistakes, resist, and are afraid. It's a slow work, so it can't be hurried, but it's urgent, so it can't be delayed. In America slow and urgent are not compatible; they cancel out each other. In the kingdom, patience and urgency are yoked together. The Christian consumer culture wants to get things done and they are looking for shortcuts to becoming like Christ, but that person God builds over a long time.

The culture is contemptuous of patience. It's the first thing they throw overboard in a storm. That storm is the mania for numbers: to build a great ministry, a great law practice, a wonderful business so we can feel affirmed, can have the resources we desire, and do it in the time frame we have planned. When this happens it creates an artificial pressure cooker. If we don't meet our expectations, we have failed. Then we must work harder and find someone to blame. I think of Paul's words to the Galatians, "Let us not become weary in doing good, for at the proper time we will reap a harvest if we do not give up" (Galatians 6:9).

Today's Exercises

Core Scripture: Mark 8:27-38

Read aloud Mark 8:27-38.

Recite this week's memory verses aloud five times.

> If anyone would come after me, he must deny himself and take up his cross and follow me. For whoever wants to save his life

will lose it, but whoever loses his life for me and for the gospel will save it (Mark 8:34-35).

Doing the Discipline: Lectio Divina

Practice the spiritual discipline of meditation via *lectio divina.*

Request to Be in His Presence

"Dear Lord, bring me into the context of Your world."

1. ***Read it***—read Mark 8:36-37 at least twice, preferably out loud.
2. ***Think it***—mull it over in your mind, thinking about the context and setting, reimagining the event, putting yourself into the situation. As you meditate, use all five senses to re-create the context and the setting by building the images that are supplied within the passages.

   List what you see, hear, feel, smell, and taste.

3. ***Pray it***—ask God to give you insight into the situation and also your life. Ask, "What is it about me that I need to deal with? What is it about me that must change?"

   Respond to what God is revealing to you by asking Him what He wants you to understand.

When you understand, respond to God by accepting and admitting whatever responsibility is implied by His revelation. State what it is that God has revealed that you must admit responsibility for doing.

4. ***Live it***—ask God to empower you to act in obedience, and to accomplish what He has revealed for you to do today.

   State what particular action(s) you will take today to accomplish what God has revealed for you to do.

Give Thanks to the Lord

"Thank You, Lord, for what You are doing in me and for what You want to accomplish in this world through me."

Journal

Record ideas, impressions, feelings, questions, and any insights you may have had during your time of meditation.

Prayer

Pray for each member of your community.

Rebuilding the Gospel from the Ground Up

DAY FIVE

Prayer

Dear Lord, teach me to be faithful. By that I mean to keep doing what You say is the right thing to do. I want to learn that I can trust that what You command me to do, when obeyed, will always be to my benefit and to Your glory. Amen.

Core Thought

The gospel values humility above celebrity.

Psychologist Robert Hogan wrote in the *Harvard Business Review* that research found humility rather than self-esteem to be the key trait of successful leaders."[2] Wouldn't it be great if the followers of Jesus believed Dr. Hogan? But what do we see? The Christian world has a highly developed celebrity system that is indistinguishable from its secular counterpart. In fact, it really isn't separate. Christian speakers and entertainers demand the same limos, dressing room cuisine, and preferential treatment as their secular colleagues.

But this is not really about the elite, who comprise less than 1 percent of the populace. Humility can be displayed by those whom society celebrates, and celebrity treatment can be demanded by people in the most humble circumstances. Circumstances do not have to control our self-image.

I (Bill) have always marveled at how easy it is to get someone to appear on television. I once hosted a local debate program on one

2. Robert Hogan quoted in "The Low Down on High Self-Esteem" by Roy F. Baumeister, *Los Angeles Times*, 25 January 2005, sec California Metro, B11.

station. I had no problem getting a congressman, pastors, and advocates to appear. There is a seductive quality about the little red light on the camera. In a culture that believes any publicity is good publicity, it is no surprise that consumer religious culture has a hunger for recognition. It begins with the small things, compliments, needing to know if we have done well, but then slips into addiction, needing affirmation, genuine or not. When we are not celebrated by others, we feel empty because we have come to use it as spiritual food.

The tendency for leaders and followers alike to celebrate themselves debilitates the Christian cause. Worship becomes about us, about our tastes, likes, and dislikes. I love the story of the person who came out of a church service complaining, "I didn't really care for that." "Good," said a friend, "because we weren't worshipping you."

The drive within us to see ourselves at the center of every song, every sermon, every event, every conversation, and every problem reminds us of our own problems. Humility removes self from center and puts God in the middle. We become a supporting player; the world and God's plan does not orbit around us.

Jesus was a man for others. As His disciples, then, our life is about others. Only then will we find ourselves. As Bonhoeffer said, "The church is only the church when it exists for others."[3] We are His disciples when we celebrate Him, not us. The gospel is about how to live; the means to learning to live is learning to die. Once you have life, Jesus says, "Now I will teach you how to give it up."

Today's Exercises

Core Scripture: Mark 8:27-38

Read aloud Mark 8:27-38.

Recite this week's memory verses aloud five times.

> If anyone would come after me, he must deny himself and take up his cross and follow me. For whoever wants to save his life

3. Dietrich Bonhoeffer, *Letters and Papers from Prison* (New York: Macmillan, 1972), 382.

will lose it, but whoever loses his life for me and for the gospel will save it (Mark 8:34-35).

Doing the Discipline: Lectio Divina

Practice the spiritual discipline of meditation via *lectio divina*.

Request to Be in His Presence

"Dear Lord, bring me into the context of Your world."

1. ***Read it***—read Mark 8:38 at least twice, preferably out loud.
2. ***Think it***—mull it over in your mind, thinking about the context and setting, reimagining the event, putting yourself into the situation. As you meditate, use all five senses to re-create the context and the setting by building the images that are supplied within the passages.

   List what you see, hear, feel, smell, and taste.

3. ***Pray it***—ask God to give you insight into the situation and also your life. Ask, "What is it about me that I need to deal with? What is it about me that must change?"

   Respond to what God is revealing to you by asking Him what He wants you to understand.

When you understand, respond to God by accepting and admitting whatever responsibility is implied by His revelation. State what it is that God has revealed that you must admit responsibility for doing.

4. ***Live it***—ask God to empower you to act in obedience, and to accomplish what He has revealed for you to do today.

   State what particular action(s) you will take today to accomplish what God has revealed for you to do.

Give Thanks to the Lord

"Thank You, Lord, for what You are doing in me and for what You want to accomplish in this world through me."

Journal

Record ideas, impressions, feelings, questions, and any insights you may have had during your time of meditation.

Prayer

Pray for each member of your community.

Rebuilding the Gospel from the Ground Up

DAY SIX

Community Meeting

In preparation for this week's meeting, you will have read and reflected upon each of the week's five Core Thoughts, recorded your thoughts and observations, and are ready to recite this week's memory verses to the group.

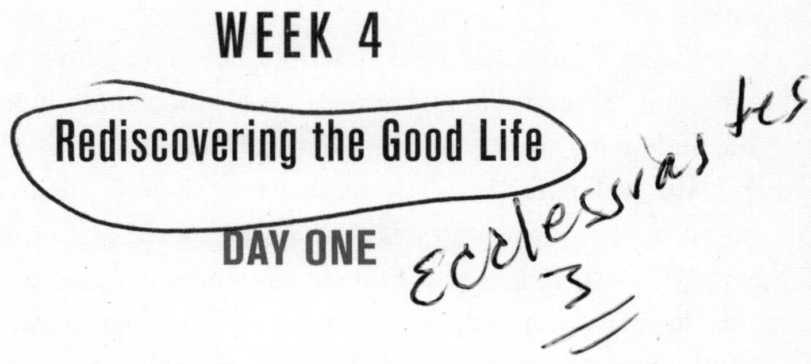

WEEK 4

Rediscovering the Good Life

DAY ONE

Prayer

Dear Lord, train me to respond in difficult times in ways that will show others that I trust myself in Your hands. Help me to display with confidence my growing trust in You as I make Your saving power present to those with whom I live, work, and play. Amen.

Core Thought

The good life is a beatific life.

Everyone wants his life to be a good life. What this usually means is that a good life makes one feel valued, elated, satisfied, safe, purposeful, and tranquil and is rewarding. Jesus believes that this notion is false. He doesn't think it false that we would feel these things in a good life but that living a life constructed to produce these feelings *is* the good life. The mistake is in thinking that having the good life, (i.e., our situation, the condition and circumstance in which we live) *causes us* to feel valued, elated, satisfied, safe, purposeful, tranquil, and rewarded. Jesus believed that our happiness should not depend on our life circumstances.

In His Sermon on the Mount (found in Matthew 5–7) Jesus teaches that those who follow Him as Lord of this new kingdom must respond differently from the way the people in this present world (which is passing away) respond. They must be "salt" and "light." They must be that "city on the hill," and let their "light shine before men," so that sinners will see their good deeds and praise their Father in heaven (i.e., be saved).

In the Beatitudes, Jesus describes how His followers in His new kingdom will carry on His restoration of all creation. From this we see the underlying reason for His followers' happiness.

The difference between those who follow Jesus and those who do not is that those who follow Jesus do not depend on their circumstances for their happiness. Their happiness is based upon the hope they have, the hope that God is making "all things new." This hope is firmly founded upon trusting in Jesus, the follower's personal experience of being renewed, and being used in the renewal of others. This trust becomes stronger as we continue to obey His commandments and accomplish His will in our lives (this is the working-out of our faith).

For the remainder of this week, each day we will examine more closely Jesus' Sermon on the Mount, especially His "beatific" sayings. Through them we can determine the behaviors that we must practice to train us to respond to suffering in ways which continue Jesus' mission to "make all things new."

Today's Exercises

Core Scripture: Matthew 5:1-16

Read aloud Matthew 5:1-16.

Recite this week's memory verse aloud five times.

> In the same way, let your light shine before men, that they may see your good deeds and praise your Father in heaven (Matthew 5:16).

Doing the Discipline: Lectio Divina

Practice the spiritual discipline of meditation via *lectio divina.*

Request to Be in His Presence

"Dear Lord, bring me into the context of Your world."

1. ***Read it***—read Matthew 5:1-3 at least twice, preferably out loud.
2. ***Think it***—mull it over in your mind, thinking about the context and setting, reimagining the event, putting yourself into the situation. As you meditate, use all five senses to re-create the context and the setting by building the images that are supplied within the passages.

   List what you see, hear, feel, smell, and taste.

3. ***Pray it***—ask God to give you insight into the situation and also your life. Ask, "What is it about me that I need to deal with? What is it about me that must change?"

   Respond to what God is revealing to you by asking Him what He wants you to understand.

   When you understand, respond to God by accepting and admitting whatever responsibility is implied by His revelation. State what it is that God has revealed that you must admit responsibility for doing.

4. ***Live it***—ask God to empower you to act in obedience, and to accomplish what He has revealed for you to do today.

   State what particular action(s) you will take today to accomplish what God has revealed for you to do.

Give Thanks to the Lord

"Thank You, Lord, for what You are doing in me and for what You want to accomplish in this world through me."

Journal

Record ideas, impressions, feelings, questions, and any insights you may have had during your time of meditation.

Prayer

Pray for each member of your community.

Rediscovering the Good Life

DAY TWO

Prayer

Dear Lord, grow in me godly character. Give me the confidence to minister not from my competency but from the power of Your Spirit within me. And let Your transforming love be known by the good that I do, that flows from the godly character You are developing in me. Amen.

Core Thought

The good life emanates from good character.

Jesus follows the Beatitudes by saying "in the same way . . . [as] the prophets before you," meaning that His followers will do the same things as the prophets did long before (Matthew 5:12). And what were the prophets doing? They were bringing God's salvation to man and suffering as the result. Jesus continues by saying that His followers are to be "salt" and "light." They should preserve (as salt does) and shine (as a light does). What we must notice are two things. First, Jesus uses only examples of things (salt, light, lamps, and bright cities) which change other things by their being *placed on* something. Secondly, their power to change comes from within them.

Salt seasons by being placed on what it seasons; if it no longer seasons it gets "trampled by men" (i.e., *under* their feet). Lamps shine brightly when they are *placed on* a stand, and a bright city is seen from all around by being *placed on* a hill. Jesus' followers are intentionally *placed on* the scene to do their work.

The salt placed on food, the lamp placed on a stand, and the bright city on a hill accomplish their work (preserving and revealing) by virtue of the power within them that is flowing out from them. The salt can preserve because the power that is within its chemical compound works when it comes into contact with food. Lamps and a city on a hill reveal and dispel darkness by virtue of their power to produce light from what is *within* them.

Jesus teaches that His followers will do His work from the power that is *within* them, what they are made of. This is the power of godly character. And this godly character will be seen by all in what they do.

This is the way people come under the transforming power of Christ. They are touched by the love of Jesus as it emanates from the godly character within His people in good deeds.

Today's Exercises

Core Scripture: Matthew 5:1-16

Read aloud Matthew 5:1-16.

Recite this week's memory verse aloud five times.

> In the same way, let your light shine before men, that they may see your good deeds and praise your Father in heaven (Matthew 5:16).

Doing the Discipline: Lectio Divina

Practice the spiritual discipline of meditation via *lectio divina.*

Request to Be in His Presence

"Dear Lord, bring me into the context of Your world."

1. ***Read it***—read Matthew 5:4-6 at least twice, preferably out loud.
2. ***Think it***—mull it over in your mind, thinking about the context and setting, reimagining the event, putting yourself into the situation. As you meditate, use all five senses to re-create the context and the setting by building the images that are supplied within the passages.

Shows how one ought to conduct his life as a Kingdom citizen

List what you see, hear, feel, smell, and taste.

Happiness comes from being Real

Recognize: my need spiritually
- Mourning when someone dies
- Gentleness extended others
- Hungrey + Thirst for Right
- Merciful

3. ***Pray it***—ask God to give you insight into the situation and also your life. Ask, "What is it about me that I need to deal with? What is it about me that must change?"

- Pure in Heart

Respond to what God is revealing to you by asking Him what He wants you to understand.

- Peacemakers
- Persecuted for Jesus

When you understand, respond to God by accepting and admitting whatever responsibility is implied by His revelation. State what it is that God has revealed that you must admit responsibility for doing.

4. ***Live it***—ask God to empower you to act in obedience, and to accomplish what He has revealed for you to do today.

   State what particular action(s) you will take today to accomplish what God has revealed for you to do.

Give Thanks to the Lord

"Thank You, Lord, for what You are doing in me and for what You want to accomplish in this world through me."

Journal

Record ideas, impressions, feelings, questions, and any insights you may have had during your time of meditation.

Prayer

Pray for each member of your community.

Rediscovering the Good Life

DAY THREE

Prayer

Dear Lord, today, use me to bless someone. Allow me to be great by being present and doing for someone what Jesus wants done. Amen.

Core Thought

The good life leads to greatness.

For Jesus and His followers, the good life (true happiness) is not found in life's circumstances. It is the product, the working-out of God's mission to "make all things new." It is produced by God's transforming/saving power and emanates from the godly character within us. As Jesus' followers live this good life, they make available to others the experience of God loving them. Through a believer's good deeds others experience God fulfilling their desire to feel valued, elated, satisfied, safe, purposeful, tranquil, and rewarded. The follower who lives the good life recognizes the great worth of others and will be recognized by others as being greatly worthy. The good life is the life that Jesus lives. It is a life lived for others. It is living the way of His kingdom now.

Today's Exercises

Core Scripture: Matthew 5:1-16

Read aloud Matthew 5:1-16.

Recite this week's memory verse aloud five times.

> In the same way, let your light shine before men, that they may see your good deeds and praise your Father in heaven (Matthew 5:16).

Doing the Discipline: Lectio Divina

Practice the spiritual discipline of meditation via *lectio divina*.

Request to Be in His Presence

"Dear Lord, bring me into the context of Your world."

1. ***Read it***—read Matthew 5:7-9 at least twice, preferably out loud.
2. ***Think it***—mull it over in your mind, thinking about the context and setting, reimagining the event, putting yourself into the situation. As you meditate, use all five senses to re-create the context and the setting by building the images that are supplied within the passages.

List what you see, hear, feel, smell, and taste.

3. ***Pray it***—ask God to give you insight into the situation and also your life. Ask, "What is it about me that I need to deal with? What is it about me that must change?"

   Respond to what God is revealing to you by asking Him what He wants you to understand.

   When you understand, respond to God by accepting and admitting whatever responsibility is implied by His revelation. State what it is that God has revealed that you must admit responsibility for doing.

4. ***Live it***—ask God to empower you to act in obedience, and to accomplish what He has revealed for you to do today.

   State what particular action(s) you will take today to accomplish what God has revealed for you to do.

Give Thanks to the Lord

"Thank You, Lord, for what You are doing in me and for what You want to accomplish in this world through me."

Journal

Record ideas, impressions, feelings, questions, and any insights you may have had during your time of meditation.

Prayer

Pray for each member of your community.

Rediscovering the Good Life

DAY FOUR

Prayer

Dear Lord, help me to find satisfaction in doing Your will because it pleases You for me to do so. I like to be recognized by others for what I do, but my real desire is to be valued for doing what I do in light of who I am becoming. Grow me into being like Jesus. In the mean time, I want You to know that I enjoy the recognition You allow me to receive for doing the things You are accomplishing through me. Amen.

Core Thought

The good life leads to a good name.

In modern western religious culture, the ultimate good (sometimes it is even called god) is found via individualism. The idea of society or community is understood as a conventional way to refer to the way groups of autonomous individuals occupy the same area because of their common circumstances. So society and community, if not accidental, are only incidental. Community is not good. Only the individuals are good. One can now see the natural conclusion that must be drawn from the modern view. Because there is nothing inherently good about community, to be a good community is to be where individuals acting *only* in their own best interests (for that is what it means to be autonomous) value other individuals (who act *only* in their own best interests) above their own best interests! Confusing? Of course it is! Because it is self-contradictory. It is nonsense!

The individualism promoted in the modern church appeals to our fallen desire for autonomy from God. We simply do not wish to be accountable to God (or anyone else for that matter) for our thoughts and actions. Now you can begin to see the dire situation in which we find ourselves.

Remember, we said that in a good life people will feel that they are valued. For the good life to be good, that desire must be fulfilled by our being provided the proper recognition that reflects our value. The dire situation is that an individual needs to be truly valued by others, not by individuals acting only in their own best interest, but by those who, quite apart from their own interests, give recognition based upon the worthiness of the person. We need to be valued (to be given a good name) by the community, but when it suits us (i.e., when we oppose the values held in common by the community). In other words, we demand that the community values us for not holding to their values. Of course this is absurd.

Our desires and needs cannot be met by the way of modern religious individualism. God provides us with the best way to the good life, where our need to be valued by others is met in the proper way. Our need for recognition is to be met within a community of people who share the Lord's beliefs. The community is called the church. And our worth will be recognized in the proper way by God through the disciples in His church as we serve one another, carrying out His kingdom's work. God intends to gloriously meet our need to be valued by Himself recognizing our worth before all men:

> His master replied, "Well done, good and faithful servant! You have been faithful with a few things; I will put you in charge of many things. Come and share your master's happiness!" (Matthew 25:23)

> When the Son of Man comes in his glory, and all the angels with him, he will sit on his throne in heavenly glory. (Matthew 25:31)

All the nations will be gathered before him . . .

Then the King will say to those on his right, "Come, you who are blessed by my Father; take your inheritance, the kingdom prepared for you since the creation of the world." (Mathew 25:32,34)

Today's Exercises

Core Scripture: Matthew 5:1-16

Read aloud Matthew 5:1-16.

Recite this week's memory verse aloud five times.

In the same way, let your light shine before men, that they may see your good deeds and praise your Father in heaven (Matthew 5:16).

Doing the Discipline: Lectio Divina

Practice the spiritual discipline of meditation via *lectio divina.*

Request to Be in His Presence

"Dear Lord, bring me into the context of Your world."

1. ***Read it***—read Matthew 5:10-12 at least twice, preferably out loud.
2. ***Think it***—mull it over in your mind, thinking about the context and setting, reimagining the event, putting yourself into the situation. As you meditate, use all five senses to re-create the context and the setting by building the images that are supplied within the passages.

List what you see, hear, feel, smell, and taste.

3. ***Pray it***—ask God to give you insight into the situation and also your life. Ask, "What is it about me that I need to deal with? What is it about me that must change?"

   Respond to what God is revealing to you by asking Him what He wants you to understand.

   When you understand, respond to God by accepting and admitting whatever responsibility is implied by His revelation. State what it is that God has revealed that you must admit responsibility for doing.

4. ***Live it***—ask God to empower you to act in obedience, and to accomplish what He has revealed for you to do today.

   State what particular action(s) you will take today to accomplish what God has revealed for you to do.

Give Thanks to the Lord

"Thank You, Lord, for what You are doing in me and for what You want to accomplish in this world through me."

Journal

Record ideas, impressions, feelings, questions, and any insights you may have had during your time of meditation.

Prayer

Pray for each member of your community.

Rediscovering the Good Life

DAY FIVE

Prayer

Dear Lord, train me to be a servant among servants. Empower me to do the things that will advance Your kingdom the way it should proceed. Help me to raise myself to the lowest position of service. Help me to trust that it will be in this position that I can be as near as I can get to Jesus. Amen.

Core Thought

The good life leads to the Good King.

What's in It for Me? may not be the hymn being sung by the worshippers in the modern, individualistic, marketing-modeled church's worship service. But it is the daily mantra being offered to the god they seek to please. Let's be very clear about this: when individualism is valued, then it is not God who is worshipped. And when churches model behaviors and attitudes that allow a culture of individualism to be valued in any way, then they are idolatrous.[1] They are promoting the worship of something other than the One, True God. Individualism promotes and is itself the practice of self-worship.

We learned that individualism cannot fulfill the need we have to be authentically valued by others. For this, God has provided a community with shared values, the church, and a common mission, the advancement of the kingdom of God in all the world. It is in the accomplishing of this common mission that each individual (as a member of Christ's

1. To worship is to recognize the value of something by behaviors that appropriately communicate its worth.

church) finds his fulfillment. By working to advance the kingdom of God, we are transformed and are becoming more like God's Son. The further we advance the kingdom, the closer we become to the King. God does not lead us to His kingdom by living the good life. It is not to a kingdom by the good life that we are being led. It is to the Good King by the good life that we are led.

Today's Exercises

Core Scripture: Matthew 5:1-16

Read aloud Matthew 5:1-16.

Recite this week's memory verse aloud five times.

> In the same way, let your light shine before men, that they may see your good deeds and praise your Father in heaven (Matthew 5:16).

Doing the Discipline: Lectio Divina

Practice the spiritual discipline of meditation via *lectio divina*.

Request to Be in His Presence

"Dear Lord, bring me into the context of Your world."

1. ***Read it***—read Matthew 5:13-16 at least twice, preferably out loud.
2. ***Think it***—mull it over in your mind, thinking about the context and setting, reimagining the event, putting yourself into the situation. As you meditate, use all five senses to re-create the context and the setting by building the images that are supplied within the passages.

List what you see, hear, feel, smell, and taste.

3. ***Pray it***—ask God to give you insight into the situation and also your life. Ask, "What is it about me that I need to deal with? What is it about me that must change?"

   Respond to what God is revealing to you by asking Him what He wants you to understand.

   When you understand, respond to God by accepting and admitting whatever responsibility is implied by His revelation. State what it is that God has revealed that you must admit responsibility for doing.

4. ***Live it***—ask God to empower you to act in obedience, and to accomplish what He has revealed for you to do today.

   State what particular action(s) you will take today to accomplish what God has revealed for you to do.

Give Thanks to the Lord

"Thank You, Lord, for what You are doing in me and for what You want to accomplish in this world through me."

Journal

Record ideas, impressions, feelings, questions, and any insights you may have had during your time of meditation.

Prayer

Pray for each member of your community.

Rediscovering the Good Life

DAY SIX

Community Meeting

In preparation for this week's meeting, you will have read and reflected upon each of the week's five Core Thoughts, recorded your thoughts and observations, and are ready to recite this week's memory verses to the group.

WEEK 5

Renewing the Mind, Part 1: Ideas

DAY ONE

Prayer

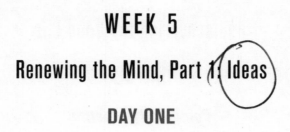

Dear Lord, I ask You to come into my mind. Please begin the process of exposing its images to the light of Your Truth. Help me not to keep albums of negative images that I was never meant to have taken. Help me to place the portrait of Your Son in its place of prominence at the center of the mantel of my mind. Amen.

Core Thought

Transformation begins with the renewing of the mind.

There is no doubt that the need for transformed minds has never been greater. There was a time when most of society held a fixed body of opinion to be true. But today we live in a philosophical jungle having many ports of origin from which people start the journey to truth. However, the desired destination for the Christian mind has never changed, that being the mind of Christ.

Personal transformation begins with the acquisition of the mind of Christ. Our minds are wired in such a way that we have thoughts that create images, feelings, and perceptions. Even spontaneous, unconscious action is based on a cognitive memory that is fixed in the mind. That is why Paul taught that transformation begins by the reprogramming of the mind (Romans 12:2). Just as every human's actions are based on what he or she thinks, one cannot conceive being like Christ without thinking like Christ.

Today's Exercises

Core Scripture: 1 Corinthians 2:6-16

Read aloud 1 Corinthians 2:6-16.

Recite this week's memory verses aloud five times.

> The Spirit searches all things, even the deep things of God. For who among men knows the thoughts of a man except the man's spirit within him? In the same way no one knows the thoughts of God except the Spirit of God. We have not received the spirit of the world but the Spirit who is from God, that we may understand what God has freely given us. (1 Corinthians 2:10-12)

Doing the Discipline: Lectio Divina

Practice the spiritual discipline of meditation via *lectio divina*.

Request to Be in His Presence

"Dear Lord, bring me into the context of Your world."

1. ***Read it***—read 1 Corinthians 2:6-7 at least twice, preferably out loud.
2. ***Think it***—mull it over in your mind, thinking about the context and setting, reimagining the event, putting yourself into the situation. As you meditate, use all five senses to re-create the context and the setting by building the images that are supplied within the passages.

List what you see, hear, feel, smell, and taste.

3. ***Pray it***—ask God to give you insight into the situation and also your life. Ask, "What is it about me that I need to deal with? What is it about me that must change?"

   Respond to what God is revealing to you by asking Him what He wants you to understand.

   When you understand, respond to God by accepting and admitting whatever responsibility is implied by His revelation. State what it is that God has revealed that you must admit responsibility for doing.

4. ***Live it***—ask God to empower you to act in obedience, and to accomplish what He has revealed for you to do today.

   State what particular action(s) you will take today to accomplish what God has revealed for you to do.

Give Thanks to the Lord

"Thank You, Lord, for what You are doing in me and for what You want to accomplish in this world through me."

Journal

Record ideas, impressions, feelings, questions, and any insights you may have had during your time of meditation.

Prayer

Pray for each member of your community.

worldly wisdom	Heavenly Wis
- Get all can	- Be satisfied w/what have
- Take care self	- Care for others
- Put Self 1st	- Put God 1st
- Humanism (Trust in man)	- Trust in God
- Get know wise Influencial	- Get know helpless Those in need

Renewing the Mind, Part 1: Ideas

DAY TWO

Prayer

Dear Lord, help me this day to keep my commitment to being Your disciple. Help me to follow and embrace the training with which I must be engaged. Grow me into the kind of spiritual athlete who no longer merely endures these exercises but has begun to enjoy the race. Amen.

Core Thought

We are called to renew our mind through training.

The transformation of the mind is not something that can be accomplished by accident or reached by simply drifting toward it. Jesus' disciples are called to choose the life and then live out the life that will renew their minds. It requires a disciplined focus and a change in the way we exercise and train our minds.

We know that the mind can be trained. Paul taught that we can rid ourselves of anxiety, for example, by following a disciplined procedure mixed with prayer (Philippians 4:6-9). Paul believed that a person could change from an anxiety-ridden, double-minded person to a peace-filled, focused, and positive-thinking disciple. But as with all significant and enduring change, it will take time.

The way God uses to renew our minds is definitely not a quick-fix approach, and like Paul, we shouldn't give up easily when we falter. As we grow in Christ and the longer we travel on the path of conforming our thinking and ideas to Christ's, this process of mind transformation will seem to become more automatic, more natural. And the more our minds are conformed to Christ's, the more our understanding will be informed by Christ. We will know God's "good, pleasing, and perfect will" (Romans 12:2).

Today's Exercises

Core Scripture: 1 Corinthians 2:6-16

Read aloud 1 Corinthians 2:6-16.

Recite this week's memory verses aloud five times.

> The Spirit searches all things, even the deep things of God. For who among men knows the thoughts of a man except the man's spirit within him? In the same way no one knows the thoughts of God except the Spirit of God. We have not received the spirit of the world but the Spirit who is from God, that we may understand what God has freely given us. (1 Corinthians 2:10-12)

Doing the Discipline: Lectio Divina

Practice the spiritual discipline of meditation via *lectio divina.*

Request to Be in His Presence

"Dear Lord, bring me into the context of Your world."

1. ***Read it***—read 1 Corinthians 2:8-9 at least twice, preferably out loud.
2. ***Think it***—mull it over in your mind, thinking about the context and setting, reimagining the event, putting yourself into the situation. As you meditate, use all five senses to re-create the context and the setting by building the images that are supplied within the passages.

List what you see, hear, feel, smell, and taste.

3. ***Pray it***—ask God to give you insight into the situation and also your life. Ask, "What is it about me that I need to deal with? What is it about me that must change?"

   Respond to what God is revealing to you by asking Him what He wants you to understand.

   When you understand, respond to God by accepting and admitting whatever responsibility is implied by His revelation. State what it is that God has revealed that you must admit responsibility for doing.

4. ***Live it***—ask God to empower you to act in obedience, and to accomplish what He has revealed for you to do today.

   State what particular action(s) you will take today to accomplish what God has revealed for you to do.

Give Thanks to the Lord

"Thank You, Lord, for what You are doing in me and for what You want to accomplish in this world through me."

Journal

Record ideas, impressions, feelings, questions, and any insights you may have had during your time of meditation.

Prayer

Pray for each member of your community.

Renewing the Mind, Part 1: Ideas

DAY THREE

Prayer

Dear Lord, I ask You to open my mind to Your ideas. Apply the fire of your Truth to the ideas and images which compose my thoughts. Cleanse the thoughts of my heart and let my feelings experience the fresh vigor of Your renewing power. Amen.

Core Thought

> The renewing of the mind begins with transforming its ideas, images, and feelings.

Our minds are packed with a conglomerate of thoughts and feelings, much of it subconscious, that inform and influence our decision-making and sometimes control our ability to submit our wills to God. These form into what we might call ideas, images, and feelings.

- Ideas are beliefs based on our life experience and worldview.
- Images are concrete and specific pictures or memories of life.
- Feelings are passions and desires we experience.[1]

Ideas are how we assign meaning to what we see and hear. Images are what the mind uses to represent ideas when it is thinking (the process of imagination). Feelings are how our bodies experience what the mind has imagined. They are sometimes referred to as the body's emotions.

---

1. Dallas Willard, *Renovation of the Heart* (Colorado Springs: NavPress, 2003), 95–140.

The mind is the intersection where ideas and images encounter the body, which feels and acts. It is here where ideas translate into action. It is where our beliefs are translated into faith. It is at this meeting that the saying "as a man thinks, so he is," is shown to be true. If to be like Christ is impossible apart from thinking like Christ, then control of the intersection (the mind) and what travels through it (our ideas, images, and feelings) is crucial.

Because the mind stands at the central intersection of our being where ideas produce action, its renewal is the crucial starting point and the primary focus for our complete transformation into Christlikeness.

Today's Exercises

Core Scripture: 1 Corinthians 2:6-16

Read aloud 1 Corinthians 2:6-16.

Recite this week's memory verses aloud five times.

> The Spirit searches all things, even the deep things of God. For who among men knows the thoughts of a man except the man's spirit within him? In the same way no one knows the thoughts of God except the Spirit of God. We have not received the spirit of the world but the Spirit who is from God, that we may understand what God has freely given us. (1 Corinthians 2:10-12)

Doing the Discipline: Lectio Divina

Practice the spiritual discipline of meditation via *lectio divina*.

Request to Be in His Presence

"Dear Lord, bring me into the context of Your world."

1. ***Read it***—read 1 Corinthians 2:10-12 at least twice, preferably out loud.
2. ***Think it***—mull it over in your mind, thinking about the context and setting, reimagining the event, putting yourself into the situation. As you meditate, use all five senses to re-create the context

and the setting by building the images that are supplied within the passages.

List what you see, hear, feel, smell, and taste.

3. ***Pray it***—ask God to give you insight into the situation and also your life. Ask, "What is it about me that I need to deal with? What is it about me that must change?"

   Respond to what God is revealing to you by asking Him what He wants you to understand.

   When you understand, respond to God by accepting and admitting whatever responsibility is implied by His revelation. State what it is that God has revealed that you must admit responsibility for doing.

4. ***Live it***—ask God to empower you to act in obedience, and to accomplish what He has revealed for you to do today.

   State what particular action(s) you will take today to accomplish what God has revealed for you to do.

Give Thanks to the Lord

"Thank You, Lord, for what You are doing in me and for what You want to accomplish in this world through me."

Journal

Record ideas, impressions, feelings, questions, and any insights you may have had during your time of meditation.

Prayer

Pray for each member of your community.

Renewing the Mind, Part 1: Ideas

DAY FOUR

Prayer

Dear Lord, show me the thoughts of my heart. Show me how they are near or far away from Yours. If far away, then break them loose from their moorings by the mighty wind of Your Spirit. And let them find no safe harbor nor strongholds in my mind to weather Your cleansing fury. Amen.

Core Thought

> The bondage of the mind begins with conforming its ideas, images, and feelings.

The mind's ideas, images, and feelings are also Satan's primary focus in his effort to thwart God's purpose. Once our minds operate with Satan's ideas according to his purposes, then he has control of our bodies and the actions they produce. This is being in bondage, gripped in the Devil's strongholds. When this occurs, he can go to work on someone else because we are completely defeated. The Bible describes these strongholds as arguments or pretensions that posture themselves as alternatives to the truth of God. In reality, despite their posturing, they are opposed to the truth of God.

Satan builds the strongholds through his effective programming of the postmodern mind. From the beginning, Satan's primary strategy was to instill in the mind the idea that God cannot be trusted to act in our best interest. So the basic message in all his temptation is, "Take charge, take what you need, and take it now." This is the pattern of the world's thinking regarding God and how we should act, knowing this to be true about Him. It's all about fear that God won't come through. We don't see God working, so we think, "I've got to do something, get something moving, take some action, produce some result." These are the slogans of minds that are conformed to the pattern of this world, the banner of those whose minds are in bondage.

Establishing strongholds in the minds of men is the Devil's method for bringing men under the bondage of fear. It is for this reason that the war for the soul is fought on the battlefield of the mind with the weapon of transformed ideas.

Today's Exercises

Core Scripture: 1 Corinthians 2:6-16

Read aloud 1 Corinthians 2:6-16.

Recite this week's memory verses aloud five times.

> The Spirit searches all things, even the deep things of God. For who among men knows the thoughts of a man except the man's spirit within him? In the same way no one knows the thoughts of God except the Spirit of God. We have not received the spirit of the world but the Spirit who is from God, that we may understand what God has freely given us. (1 Corinthians 2:10-12)

Doing the Discipline: Lectio Divina

Practice the spiritual discipline of meditation via *lectio divina*.

Request to Be in His Presence

"Dear Lord, bring me into the context of Your world."

1. ***Read it***—read 1 Corinthians 2:13-14 at least twice, preferably out loud.
2. ***Think it***—mull it over in your mind, thinking about the context and setting, reimagining the event, putting yourself into the situation. As you meditate, use all five senses to re-create the context

and the setting by building the images that are supplied within the passages.

List what you see, hear, feel, smell, and taste.

3. ***Pray it***—ask God to give you insight into the situation and also your life. Ask, "What is it about me that I need to deal with? What is it about me that must change?"

   Respond to what God is revealing to you by asking Him what He wants you to understand.

   When you understand, respond to God by accepting and admitting whatever responsibility is implied by His revelation. State what it is that God has revealed that you must admit responsibility for doing.

4. ***Live it***—ask God to empower you to act in obedience, and to accomplish what He has revealed for you to do today.

   State what particular action(s) you will take today to accomplish what God has revealed for you to do.

Give Thanks to the Lord

"Thank You, Lord, for what You are doing in me and for what You want to accomplish in this world through me."

Journal

Record ideas, impressions, feelings, questions, and any insights you may have had during your time of meditation.

Prayer

Pray for each member of your community.

Renewing the Mind, Part 1: Ideas

DAY FIVE

Prayer

Dear Lord, I want to be like Jesus. I know that I don't even understand much of what it means to be like Jesus. For this reason, I ask You to help me train my mind to be like His and my heart to desire what He desires. Amen.

Core Thought

> God renews our mind by dislodging false ideas and establishing new ideas.

The renewing of our mind is the process of dislodging and disposing of the false ideas which reflect the values of this fallen world. But renewal is not complete until the grave left in the mind from removing its false ideas is filled in with a solid soil of ideas based upon God's revealed truth. For example, though we may have grown accustomed to being in bondage, having our own ideas based in fear and lack of trust, we have the antidote in the healing words of Scripture which bring about our release and redemption from bondage. We are told:

> Trust in the Lord with all your heart and lean not on your own understanding; in all your ways acknowledge him, and he will make your paths straight. (Proverbs 3:5-6)

> Do not let your hearts be troubled. Trust in God; trust also in me [Jesus]. (John 14:1)

> God is our refuge and strength, an ever-present help in trouble. Therefore we will not fear. (Psalm 46:1-2)

> No temptation has seized you except what is common to man. And God is faithful; he will not let you be tempted beyond what you can bear. But when you are tempted, he will also provide a way out so that you can stand up under it. (1 Corinthians 10:13)

By living in God's renewing power, we can dislodge and destroy the strongholds of even long-held false beliefs.

Through the process of transformation, we establish within our minds new life-giving, life-affirming ideas, such as the truths listed above. With these new ideas in a mind that conforms its manner of thinking after the mind of Christ, we live the new life, the way of Jesus. It is the life of an easy yoke and a light burden.

Today's Exercises

Core Scripture: 1 Corinthians 2:6-16

Read aloud 1 Corinthians 2:6-16.

Recite this week's memory verses aloud five times.

> The Spirit searches all things, even the deep things of God. For who among men knows the thoughts of a man except the man's spirit within him? In the same way no one knows the thoughts of God except the Spirit of God. We have not received the spirit of the world but the Spirit who is from God, that we may understand what God has freely given us. (1 Corinthians 2:10-12)

Doing the Discipline: Lectio Divina

Practice the spiritual discipline of meditation via *lectio divina*.

Request to Be in His Presence

"Dear Lord, bring me into the context of Your world."

1. ***Read it***—read 1 Corinthians 2:15-16 at least twice, preferably out loud.
2. ***Think it***—mull it over in your mind, thinking about the context and setting, reimagining the event, putting yourself into the situation. As you meditate, use all five senses to re-create the context and the setting by building the images that are supplied within the passages.

   List what you see, hear, feel, smell, and taste.

3. ***Pray it***—ask God to give you insight into the situation and also your life. Ask, "What is it about me that I need to deal with? What is it about me that must change?"

   Respond to what God is revealing to you by asking Him what He wants you to understand.

   When you understand, respond to God by accepting and admitting whatever responsibility is implied by His revelation. State what it is that God has revealed that you must admit responsibility for doing.

4. ***Live it***—ask God to empower you to act in obedience, and to accomplish what He has revealed for you to do today.

   State what particular action(s) you will take today to accomplish what God has revealed for you to do.

Give Thanks to the Lord

"Thank You, Lord, for what You are doing in me and for what You want to accomplish in this world through me."

Journal

Record ideas, impressions, feelings, questions, and any insights you may have had during your time of meditation.

Prayer

Pray for each member of your community.

Renewing the Mind, Part 1: Ideas

DAY SIX

Community Meeting

In preparation for this week's meeting, you will have read and reflected upon each of the week's five Core Thoughts, recorded your thoughts and observations, and are ready to recite this week's memory verses to the group.

WEEK 6

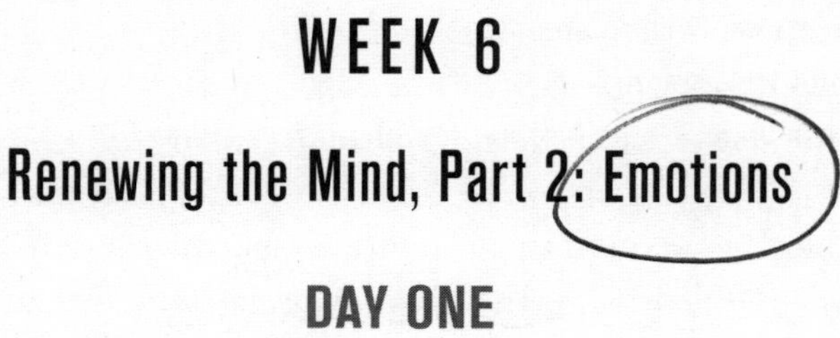

Renewing the Mind, Part 2: Emotions

DAY ONE

Prayer

Dear Lord, I want to have the mind of Christ. I know that there are things that my mind uses to direct my choices. I want to make sure that what my mind uses will direct my choices toward accomplishing Your will. I am not confident that my thinking is built upon the solid ground of Your Truth. Please help me examine my heart and mind. I want them to be in total agreement with Yours. Amen.

Core Thought

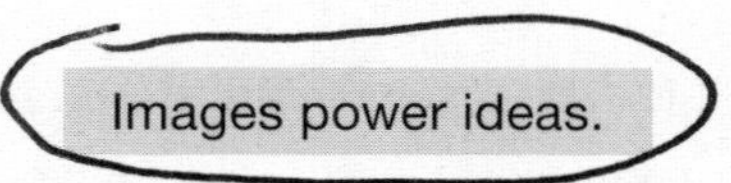

Images power ideas.

Images are the pictures in our mind's eye. They are concrete and often specific. The images that accompany our ideas make them more powerful. Images call into our consciousness the ideals, the values, and the passions that a particular image represents. They are what the Lincoln Memorial is to liberty, what Lance Armstrong is to dedication, and what Elvis Presley is to self-indulgence. Images are formed daily by the onslaught of media and information overload that crowd into our lives.

Because most of our images are constructed from the impressions we perceive as we experience ourselves in the world, we should expect that they suffer from the same distortion as our ideas of being conformed to the pattern of this world. This means that to have the mind of Christ, we must engage in behaviors (like *Lectio Divina*) that will renew the images that our mind uses to direct our thinking.

Today's Exercises

Core Scripture: Philippians 4:6-13

Read aloud Philippians 4:6-13.

Recite this week's memory verses aloud five times.

> Do not be anxious about anything, but in everything, by prayer and petition, with thanksgiving, present your requests to God. And the peace of God, which transcends all understanding, will guard your hearts and your minds in Christ Jesus. (Philippians 4:6-7)

Doing the Discipline: Lectio Divina

Practice the spiritual discipline of meditation via *lectio divina*.

Request to Be in His Presence

"Dear Lord, bring me into the context of Your world."

1. ***Read it***—read Philippians 4:6-7 at least twice, preferably out loud.
2. ***Think it***—mull it over in your mind, thinking about the context and setting, reimagining the event, putting yourself into the situation. As you meditate, use all five senses to re-create the context and the setting by building the images that are supplied within the passages.

List what you see, hear, feel, smell, and taste.

3. ***Pray it***—ask God to give you insight into the situation and also your life. Ask, "What is it about me that I need to deal with? What is it about me that must change?"

   Respond to what God is revealing to you by asking Him what He wants you to understand.

   When you understand, respond to God by accepting and admitting whatever responsibility is implied by His revelation. State what it is that God has revealed that you must admit responsibility for doing.

4. ***Live it***—ask God to empower you to act in obedience, and to accomplish what He has revealed for you to do today.

   State what particular action(s) you will take today to accomplish what God has revealed for you to do.

Give Thanks to the Lord

"Thank You, Lord, for what You are doing in me and for what You want to accomplish in this world through me."

Journal

Record ideas, impressions, feelings, questions, and any insights you may have had during your time of meditation.

Prayer

Pray for each member of your community.

Renewing the Mind, Part 2: Emotions

DAY TWO

Prayer

Dear Lord, I do not want to be hindered in my service to You. Help me to continue to cleanse my heart and mind through its encounter with the Truth of Your Word. Amen.

Core Thought

Distorted images empower ideas.

Our ability to imagine is a product of being made in God's likeness. We create images in our mind by using only our mind to call them instantly into existence. We can manipulate and animate them anyway we choose.

Just as images can be powerfully used for good, they can also magnify negatives. One's negative image of self can override clear thinking or any other force in life. For example, Karen Carpenter, the once-great singer who lost her struggle with an eating disorder, starved herself to death based on a false image. What she saw in the mirror was a lie, but that image had tremendous power. It did not override her ability to freely choose. Rather it so forcefully presented its distorted picture of reality that it supplied her already developed and disciplined will with the fortitude to ignore all the self-inflicted pain she was feeling, to disregard all the sound advice her loved ones offered, and subject herself to its lie. This shows that images derive their power from the strength of a good mind.

The stronger the mind, the more powerfully its images will influence its thinking. Once a strong mind's imagination falls subject to the delusions caused by distorted images, it can only be rescued by another more powerful Mind, One untainted by distorted images and incapable of being deceived.

Thanks be to the Father, who has placed within us His Holy Spirit, the One who will guide us into all truth.

Today's Exercises

Core Scripture: Philippians 4:6-13

Read aloud Philippians 4:6-13.

Recite this week's memory verses aloud five times.

> Do not be anxious about anything, but in everything, by prayer and petition, with thanksgiving, present your requests to God. And the peace of God, which transcends all understanding, will guard your hearts and your minds in Christ Jesus. (Philippians 4:6-7)

Doing the Discipline: Lectio Divina

Practice the spiritual discipline of meditation via *lectio divina*.

Request to Be in His Presence

"Dear Lord, bring me into the context of Your world."

1. ***Read it***—read Philippians 4:8 at least twice, preferably out loud.
2. ***Think it***—mull it over in your mind, thinking about the context and setting, reimagining the event, putting yourself into the situation. As you meditate, use all five senses to re-create the context and the setting by building the images that are supplied within the passages.

List what you see, hear, feel, smell, and taste.

3. ***Pray it***—ask God to give you insight into the situation and also your life. Ask, "What is it about me that I need to deal with? What is it about me that must change?"

   Respond to what God is revealing to you by asking Him what He wants you to understand.

   When you understand, respond to God by accepting and admitting whatever responsibility is implied by His revelation. State what it is that God has revealed that you must admit responsibility for doing.

4. ***Live it***—ask God to empower you to act in obedience, and to accomplish what He has revealed for you to do today.

   State what particular action(s) you will take today to accomplish what God has revealed for you to do.

Give Thanks to the Lord

"Thank You, Lord, for what You are doing in me and for what You want to accomplish in this world through me."

Journal

Record ideas, impressions, feelings, questions, and any insights you may have had during your time of meditation.

Prayer

Pray for each member of your community.

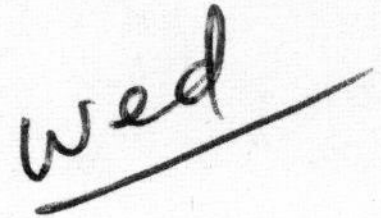

Renewing the Mind, Part 2: Emotions

DAY THREE

Prayer

Dear Lord, thank You for the cleansing power of Your Word upon my mind. I offer my ideas and images to Your refining fire. Please make me holy. Amen.

Core Thought

God's Word transforms distorted images.

A wrong idea accompanied by a powerful image will distort discernment. This is why A. W. Tozer's statement is so relevant: "Whatever comes into your mind when you think about God is the most important thing about you."[1]

The transformation of the mind must include first our ideas and second the images that give them power. That is why the cornerstone for the transformation of the mind lies in reading, meditating on, and memorizing the Scriptures along with time in silence and solitude. It is largely through these disciplines that you begin to take on new ideas with accompanying images.

The ideas and images that need to be transformed are deeply embedded, so the Scriptures will need to go just as deep. It is an acquired skill to go deep, to reroute the words through the heart in prayer and reflection. So we rebuild the mind slowly, idea by idea, passage by passage, until the ideas of Christ crowd out and replace the destructive fixtures that have held us captive. It is a good habit to pray along the following

1. A. W. Tozer, *Knowledge of the Holy* (San Francisco: Harper, 1998), 9.

lines when faced with a crisis or a major decision: "Lord, what lies have I believed, what images of myself and others are distorted? Lord, bring down those strongholds." This prayer is best said on one's knees with an open Bible, for the answers lie in prayer and meditation on God's Word.

Today's Exercises

Core Scripture: Philippians 4:6-13

Read aloud Philippians 4:6-13.

Recite this week's memory verses aloud five times.

> Do not be anxious about anything, but in everything, by prayer and petition, with thanksgiving, present your requests to God. And the peace of God, which transcends all understanding, will guard your hearts and your minds in Christ Jesus. (Philippians 4:6-7)

Doing the Discipline: Lectio Divina

Practice the spiritual discipline of meditation via *lectio divina.*

Request to Be in His Presence

"Dear Lord, bring me into the context of Your world."

1. ***Read it***—read Philippians 4:9 at least twice, preferably out loud.
2. ***Think it***—mull it over in your mind, thinking about the context and setting, reimagining the event, putting yourself into the situation. As you meditate, use all five senses to re-create the context and the setting by building the images that are supplied within the passages.

List what you see, hear, feel, smell, and taste.

3. ***Pray it***—ask God to give you insight into the situation and also your life. Ask, "What is it about me that I need to deal with? What is it about me that must change?"

   Respond to what God is revealing to you by asking Him what He wants you to understand.

   When you understand, respond to God by accepting and admitting whatever responsibility is implied by His revelation. State what it is that God has revealed that you must admit responsibility for doing.

4. ***Live it***—ask God to empower you to act in obedience, and to accomplish what He has revealed for you to do today.

   State what particular action(s) you will take today to accomplish what God has revealed for you to do.

Give Thanks to the Lord

"Thank You, Lord, for what You are doing in me and for what You want to accomplish in this world through me."

Journal

Record ideas, impressions, feelings, questions, and any insights you may have had during your time of meditation.

Prayer

Pray for each member of your community.

Renewing the Mind, Part 2: Emotions

DAY FOUR

Prayer

Dear Lord, today, help me to examine my emotions. I know You designed me with emotions, so I know that they can be used to glorify You. Teach me how my emotions can properly honor You. Amen.

Core Thought

Renewing the mind transforms the emotions.

Transformation of the mind begins with the renewing of the mind's ideas and the images that call them into play and empower their influence upon the mind's thinking. When the mind communicates the power of these ideas and the images that carry them, they are experienced by the body as what we call feelings or emotions. This is how God designed our mind to process our ideas.

Once emotions are produced and begin to be expressed by the body, they are the most powerful force the mind can exert in the physical world. This bodily expression of the mind or heart was designed to be used in the worshipping of God and to express our love for one another. However, when sin corrupts our ideas and distorts the images which bear them, our emotions no longer function solely according to how God intended. A biblical example of this is the story of God's counsel to Cain when he grew angry at God's rejection of his offering.

> Then the LORD said to Cain, "Why are you angry? Why is your face downcast? If you do what is right, will you not be accepted? But if you do not do what is right, sin is crouching

> at your door; it desires to have you, but you must master it." (Genesis 4:6-7)

God's counsel to Cain was, if you do right, you will feel right.

Feelings are the product of right ideas and images, connected to right behavior. Cain's actions were based on the *wrong* idea that he could please God on his own terms and supported by the image that God would smile upon him, which led to powerful feelings of rejection. Cain's expectations were not met, so he became angry and malice filled his heart. God told him what to do and warned him that if he didn't master his feelings and resist what he was thinking of doing, evil would have its way with him. Cain did not master his emotions. His emotions propelled his actions that led him to murder his brother, and just as God had warned, evil then became his master.

We must be the master of our emotions. This does not necessarily mean that we are to suppress their expression. What it does mean is that our emotions are to be directed by our minds to perform their expressive function in accordance to God's design. They are to be the instruments that express our experience of what is true about God, ourselves, and the world. To renew them is to restore them to their proper place and function, under the direction of a mind that is being renewed by the Spirit of God.

Today's Exercises

Core Scripture: Philippians 4:6-13

Read aloud Philippians 4:6-13.

Recite this week's memory verses aloud five times.

> Do not be anxious about anything, but in everything, by prayer and petition, with thanksgiving, present your requests to God. And the peace of God, which transcends all understanding, will guard your hearts and your minds in Christ Jesus. (Philippians 4:6-7)

Doing the Discipline: Lectio Divina

Practice the spiritual discipline of meditation via *lectio divina.*

Request to Be in His Presence

"Dear Lord, bring me into the context of Your world."

1. ***Read it***—read Philippians 4:10-11 at least twice, preferably out loud.
2. ***Think it***—mull it over in your mind, thinking about the context and setting, reimagining the event, putting yourself into the situation. As you meditate, use all five senses to re-create the context and the setting by building the images that are supplied within the passages.

   List what you see, hear, feel, smell, and taste.

3. ***Pray it***—ask God to give you insight into the situation and also your life. Ask, "What is it about me that I need to deal with? What is it about me that must change?"

   Respond to what God is revealing to you by asking Him what He wants you to understand.

When you understand, respond to God by accepting and admitting whatever responsibility is implied by His revelation. State what it is that God has revealed that you must admit responsibility for doing.

4. ***Live it***—ask God to empower you to act in obedience, and to accomplish what He has revealed for you to do today.

   State what particular action(s) you will take today to accomplish what God has revealed for you to do.

Give Thanks to the Lord

"Thank You, Lord, for what You are doing in me and for what You want to accomplish in this world through me."

Journal

Record ideas, impressions, feelings, questions, and any insights you may have had during your time of meditation.

Prayer

Pray for each member of your community.

Renewing the Mind, Part 2: Emotions

DAY FIVE

Prayer

Dear Lord, help me to train my emotions to be subject to the mind of Christ. Let them find their rightful place of expression under the control of the sound mind You are building within me. Amen.

Core Thought

Emotions are renewed by placing them in subjection to a renewed mind.

Feelings are powerful; they can and do overwhelm us. Sometimes we need our emotions to flow freely. Willpower will not conquer feelings; we are almost helpless in their path. Passions and desires, as the Bible calls them, are the most used and powerful tools that trigger sinful action. We are exhorted to put away such strong urges (Galatians 5:19-21). This affects without regard both young and old. People of all ages can be enslaved to their feelings of anger, anxiety, malice, rage, lust, and bitterness.

Rather than try to control or stuff emotions, God says we can change them: "Those who belong to Christ Jesus have crucified the sinful nature with its passions and desires" (Galatians 5:24). So what is required is crucifixion.

There are two crucifixions needed. The first one we experienced mysteriously and passively in Christ when we entered into His provision of eternal life (Romans 6:6). The second requires our active participation as we existentially live that first crucifixion day by day, taking every thought captive to Christ, working out what God has worked in us, and walking in the light and the Spirit (2 Corinthians 10:3-5; Galatians 5:16-17; Ephesians 5:15–6:4; Philippians 2:13; 1 John 1:3-9).

There is some good news. It is that our emotions can become servants and no longer our masters. Healthy feelings—joy, humor, delighting in God—are essential to the good life. They don't just happen, though. We must train our emotions to be our servants, serving at the disposal of the Spirit that lives within us.

Today's Exercises

Core Scripture: Philippians 4:6-13

Read aloud Philippians 4:6-13.

Recite this week's memory verses aloud five times.

> Do not be anxious about anything, but in everything, by prayer and petition, with thanksgiving, present your requests to God. And the peace of God, which transcends all understanding, will guard your hearts and your minds in Christ Jesus. (Philippians 4:6-7)

Doing the Discipline: Lectio Divina

Practice the spiritual discipline of meditation via *lectio divina*.

Request to Be in His Presence

"Dear Lord, bring me into the context of Your world."

1. ***Read it***—read Philippians 4:12-13 at least twice, preferably out loud.
2. ***Think it***—mull it over in your mind, thinking about the context and setting, reimagining the event, putting yourself into the situation. As you meditate, use all five senses to re-create the context and the setting by building the images that are supplied within the passages.

List what you see, hear, feel, smell, and taste.

3. ***Pray it***—ask God to give you insight into the situation and also your life. Ask, "What is it about me that I need to deal with? What is it about me that must change?"

   Respond to what God is revealing to you by asking Him what He wants you to understand.

   When you understand, respond to God by accepting and admitting whatever responsibility is implied by His revelation. State what it is that God has revealed that you must admit responsibility for doing.

4. ***Live it***—ask God to empower you to act in obedience, and to accomplish what He has revealed for you to do today.

   State what particular action(s) you will take today to accomplish what God has revealed for you to do.

Give Thanks to the Lord

"Thank You, Lord, for what You are doing in me and for what You want to accomplish in this world through me."

Journal

Record ideas, impressions, feelings, questions, and any insights you may have had during your time of meditation.

Prayer

Pray for each member of your community.

Renewing the Mind, Part 2: Emotions

DAY SIX

Community Meeting

In preparation for this week's meeting, you will have read and reflected upon each of the week's five Core Thoughts, recorded your thoughts and observations, and are ready to recite this week's memory verses to the group.

APPENDIX ONE

Experience the Life Community Purpose and Covenant

Our community's purpose is:

To *develop relationships with one another* that will help support and encourage each of us *to grow in Christlikeness* through *loving one another* by *sharing* our thoughts, experiences, concerns, fears, successes, and failures and by *serving* one another when a need or the opportunity arises as we *experience the life* in response to Jesus' call to "be transformed by the renewing of [our minds]" (Romans 12:2).

Therefore, I commit, for the next ______ weeks, to accomplishing our purpose by:

- making my spiritual growth and relationship with God one of my top three priorities (with spouse and family)
- completing the daily readings and exercises on time, each week
- being faithful in my attendance to community meetings (only injury, sickness, family, and work schedule conflicts are reasonable excuses for absences) and calling prior to our weekly meeting to inform our leader of my absence
- participating in discussion, prayer, and the sharing of ideas
- being honest and open when I share my thoughts and feelings
- maintaining complete confidentiality of anything discussed in our group by our members (unless prior permission to disclose the information has been given by all the individuals involved), and
- Praying daily for each member of the community and the needs they have shared.

Name: ________________________________

Date: ____________

APPENDIX TWO

Catching Up

(for those who are latecomers to an ETL community)

If you are joining an Experience the Life Community that has already completed the first week in the ETL course (Book One: *Believe as Jesus Believed,* Week One) taking the following steps will help you to catch up.

- Read this book's "Introduction" and "About this Book."
- Read and sign the Experience the Life: Community Purpose and Covenant (found in Appendix One of Book One), and bring it to your next community meeting.
- View the course DVDs for each week you have missed. Answer the corresponding questions (found under the *Experience the Life* section in Discussion Questions) for Day Six of the previous week.
- Learn how to practice the spiritual discipline of meditation by *Lectio Divina* by reading the Discovering the Discipline section for each day of Week One in Book One.

LEADER'S GUIDE

PREPARING FOR THE FIRST MEETING

Community: Assembling the Members

The first order of business is to determine the members, size, and makeup of the community.

The community should consist of:

- **Members:** all believers

  While no particular age range or level of spiritual maturity or Christian experience should be the overarching criterion for inclusion in your community, given that the objectives of EXPERIENCE THE LIFE are only obtainable by Christians, it is assumed that each member of any particular EXPERIENCE THE LIFE Community is already a Christian.

- **Makeup:** two to six members (optimally)

  The book can also be used as a discussion guide for leading larger groups through an exploration of EXPERIENCE THE LIFE (see About This Book, Its Pattern).

- **Materials:** the book

  Once the membership of the community is established, each member should acquire a copy of Book One, *Believe as Jesus Believed: Transformed Mind,* and have the course DVDs available for viewing. The books must be available to each member at least one week prior to the first community meeting.

This brings us to the second order of business: *when* and *where* the community will meet.

Calendar

The members of the community need to establish when and where the community will have its weekly meeting. Bear in mind that it will require about 90 minutes from start to finish to accomplish all that is to be done at the community meeting. What matters most in setting the time of these meetings is that all of the members are able to make this accommodation. As you will learn in the course of this journey, the commitment to community is essential to your own personal transformation. Therefore it is imperative that all members be present and able to contribute each time the community meets.

In selecting the location of your meeting, choose a site that will allow for the fewest possible interruptions, confidential conversation, and ease of access. After consensus is reached, write your name and date in the appropriate space provided on your Covenant (see Appendix One).

Commitment

Having determined the community's membership, meeting location, and time, the newly formed community needs to clearly state, and each member needs to affirm, their commitment to accomplishing what is stated in their Purpose and Covenant. We have included a covenant (see Appendix One), and each member should read, sign, and turn in the Covenant to the organizer/leader of their community at their first community meeting.

What about those who wish to join your community after it has already begun? Latecomers may join as long as they fulfill the same requirements as have the current members. Instruct the latecomer to complete the steps in Appendix Two: "Catch Up" for those who are latecomers to an ETL community.

The final order of business in preparation for your first community meeting is for each community member to read the Introduction and About This Book sections in this book and write their answers for each of the questions posed in The First Community Meeting.

THE FIRST COMMUNITY MEETING

In preparation for this week's meeting, all community members will have:

- Read the "Introduction" and "About This Book" sections in Book One: *Believe as Jesus Believed* and have written their answers to each of the questions posed below (in Questions for Discussion).
- Read and signed the Experience the Life: Community Purpose and Covenant and brought it to the meeting.
- Reflected upon the ideas and concepts presented in the readings, recorded their thoughts and observations, and are ready to share them with the group.
- Prayed that God would begin to build in them a strong and growing commitment to participate in, understand, and accomplish all the different things that EXPERIENCE THE LIFE will use these next thirty weeks, to transform them from who they are into who they are to be in Christ.

Questions for Discussion

Write your answers to the following questions:

1. Why does our mind need renovation?

2. How does our being in community provide the spiritual traction necessary for our transformation?

At This Week's Meeting

3. Open this session by asking God to help each one in attendance to be slow to speak, eager to listen, open to hear others' thoughts, to entertain one another's ideas, and to share what God is doing with them in the process of their being transformed.

4. Briefly discuss the answers members have for the questions above. Allow members to briefly share any insights, questions, or illumination they have resulting from the readings.

Discovering the Discipline: Lectio Divina

5. Read aloud to your group the following introduction to the practice of this week's spiritual discipline.

The discipline of meditation is foundational to the transformation of our thinking. We discipline our mind to return to God throughout the day, and specifically we focus our thinking on a verse, passage, thought, or image presented from Scripture. The goal here is not Bible study, where we seek to establish the meaning of the text. Rather, in meditation we listen for insight into its meaning where we internalize and personalize the passage.

Meditation is not about an empty mind. It is about filling the mind with God's thoughts. It can employ all five senses as we imagine the gospel stories. Richard Foster gives an example in his book *Celebration of Discipline:*

> Take a single event like the resurrection, or a parable, or a few verses, or even a single word and allow it to take root in you. Seek to live the experience, remembering the encouragement of Ignatius of Loyola to apply all our senses to the task. Smell the sea. Hear the lap of water along the shore. See the crowd. Feel the sun on your head and the hunger in your stomach. Taste the salt in the air. Touch the hem of His garment. Francis de Sales has instructed us to ". . . represent to your imagination

the whole of the mystery on which you desire to meditate as if it really passed in your presence . . . and that you being there, behold and hear all that was done and said."[1]

Discussing the Discipline

As a group, discuss the following questions:

6. What do you see as the possible benefits of engaging in the form of meditation being recommended by Foster?

7. What are some possible pitfalls that we should guard against?

Doing the Discipline: The Practice of Lectio Divina

8. Beginning on Day One of Week One, we will learn and practice biblical meditation using the method called *Lectio Divina*.[2]

---

1. Richard Foster, *Celebration of Discipline* (New York: Harper and Row, 1978), 26.
2. We have drawn on much of what Eugene Peterson has written to develop this method of practicing *Lectio Divina*; see especially his treatment in *Eat This Book*.

The *Lectio Divina* or "divine-reading" method that we will learn employs the four elements for divine-reading of Holy Scripture.

In Day One's session, we will learn what *Lectio Divina* (hence called LD) is and how and why it is different from other reading methods.

For the remainder of the week, each day will introduce one of LD's four ways of reading and employ it in that day's time of meditation. A particular passage from Scripture for each week has been provided on which to meditate.

For the remaining five weeks of Book One, allow *at least* ten minutes of uninterrupted time each day to engage in the discipline of meditation. This may be done at any time during the day, not necessarily at the same time you are completing the daily regimen.

Experience the Life

9. Play the ETL Course DVD "*Book One: Believe as Jesus Believed*," "Week One: Redrawing Your Brain Map."

Discussion Questions

As a group, discuss the ideas that Bill Hull introduced and answer the question below.

10. Why do we need our mind's map redrawn?

Close

11. Share matters for the community to pray about through the following week. Pray to close the meeting.

When leading a larger group through EXPERIENCE THE LIFE, keep in mind that most of the spiritual traction for transformation is due to the interaction that the Lord has with each individual through the other individuals in a community of believers. To preserve this traction, the leader must provide a venue and time for this interaction. For this reason, we suggest that some time during the weekly session, the leader divide the large group into smaller groups mimicking the two- to six-member community group for the purpose of more intimately discussing the issues presented in the week's session. It is reported after experiencing successive weeks with the same members of this smaller discussion group, individuals previously not participants in a small-group program have desired to continue in such a program.

While we believe that the most effective and efficient means of leading individuals to healthy spiritual transformation is in the context of a smaller community group, we do acknowledge that the larger group setting may be the only means currently available to a church's leadership. Though the *form* of instruction is important, the *function* is what must be preserved: *Verum supremus vultus* (truth above form).

WEEK 1

Redrawing Your Brain Map
Community Meeting

DAY SIX

In preparation for this week's meeting, you will have read and reflected upon each of the week's five Core Thoughts, recorded your thoughts and observations, and are ready to recite this week's memory verses to the group.

At This Week's Meeting

1. Open this session by asking God to help each one be aware of His gracious presence.
2. Have each member a turn reciting to the group this week's memory verse.
3. Discuss this week's Core Thoughts; that change is:
   a. a choice,
   b. a new mental map,
   c. crashing through the brain barriers,
   d. rejecting a common false belief,
   e. acquiring the common true beliefs.
4. Allow members to briefly share any insights, questions, or illumination they have resulting from this week's daily readings and exercises.

Discovering the Discipline

5. Read aloud to your group the following about the spiritual discipline of meditation.

Meditation

[When we study the Word of God] we not only read and hear and inquire, but we *meditate* on what comes before us; that is, we withdraw into silence where we prayerfully and steadily focus upon it. In this way its meaning for us can emerge and form us as God works in the depths of our heart, mind, and soul. We devote long periods of time to this. Our prayer as we study meditatively is always that God would meet with us and speak specifically to us, for ultimately the Word of God is God speaking.[3]

Discussing the Discipline

6. As a group, discuss the following questions:

   Why, and in what ways should we read Scripture differently from how we read, for instance, our daily newspaper?

7. How do you suppose you would be changed (be different) if you continue to make this kind of meditative practice (*Lectio Divina*) a regular part of your life?

---

3. Dallas Willard, *Spirit of the Disciplines* (San Francisco: Harper and Row, 1992), 177.

Experience the Life

8. Play the ETL course DVD "Week 2: Recovering a Biblical Faith."

Discussion Questions

9. As a group, discuss the ideas that Bill Hull introduced, and answer the question below.

   What was meant by the statement "we have been saved by grace and paralyzed by it too"? In what sense is this true?

Close

10. Share matters for the community to pray about through the following week. Pray to close the meeting.

WEEK 2

Recovering Biblical Faith Community Meeting

DAY SIX

In preparation for this week's meeting, you will have read, reflected upon each of the week's five Core Thoughts, recorded your thoughts and observations, and are ready to recite this week's memory verse to the group.

At This Week's Meeting

1. Open this session by asking God to help us to truly hear one another, and to listen carefully for His voice in all that will be said.
2. Have each member take a turn reciting to the group this week's memory verse.
3. Discuss this week's Core Thoughts, that biblical faith is:
   a. perfected by obedience,
   b. performed by hearing and obeying,
   c. persistence in prayer,
   d. patiently following where Jesus leads, and
   e. proceeding with confidence.
4. Allow members to briefly share any insights, questions, illumination, etc., they have resulting from this week's exercises.

Discovering the Discipline: Lectio Divina

5. Read aloud to your group the following regarding meditation.

   The simplest and most basic way to meditate upon the text of Scripture is through the imagination. In this regard, Alexander Whyte speaks of "the divine offices and the splendid services of the Christian imagination." Perhaps some rare individuals can experience God through abstract meditation alone, but most of us need to be more deeply rooted in the senses.

This is a wonderful aid as we come to the text of Scripture. We are desiring to see, to hear, to touch the biblical narrative. In this simple way we begin to enter the story and make it our own. We move from detached observation to active participation.

We must not despise this simpler, more humble route into God's presence. Jesus himself taught in this manner, making constant appeal to the imagination in his parables. Many of the devotional masters likewise encourage us in this way. Saint Teresa of Avila says, "As I could not make reflection with my understanding I contrived to picture Christ within me. I did many simple things of this kind. I believe my soul gained very much in this way, because I began to practice prayer without knowing what it was." Many of us can identify with her words, for we, too, have tried a merely cerebral approach and found it too mechanical, too detached.

Even more, the imagination helps to anchor our thoughts and center our attention. Francis de Sales notes that "by means of the imagination we confine our mind within the mystery on which we meditate, that it may not ramble to and fro, just as we shut up a bird in a cage or tie a hawk by his leash so that he may rest on the hand."

Using the imagination also brings the emotions into the equation, so that we come to God with both mind and heart.[4]

4. Richard Foster, *Prayer* (San Francisco: Harper Collins, 1992), 147.

Discussing the Discipline

6. As a group, share what you experienced this week as you engaged in the practice of meditating upon God's Word, using the method *Lectio Divina*.

7. What actions did God's Spirit prompt you to take as He spoke to you this week?

Experience the Life

8. Play the ETL Course DVD "Week Three: Rebuilding the Gospel."

Discussion Questions

9. As a group, discuss the ideas that Bill Hull introduced, and answer the question below.

   What is the "forgiveness-only gospel," the "gospel of the left," the "gospel of prosperity," and the "consumer gospel"? What is wrong with each of them?

Close

10. Share matters for the community to pray about through the following week. Pray to close the meeting.

WEEK 3

Rebuilding the Gospel from the Ground Up Community Meeting

DAY SIX

In preparation for this week's meeting, you will have read and reflected upon each of the week's five Core Thoughts, recorded your thoughts and observations, and are ready to recite this week's memory verses to the group.

At This Week's Meeting

1. Open this session by asking God to help us to truly hear one another and to listen carefully for His voice in all that will be said.
2. Have each member take a turn reciting to the group this week's memory verse.
3. Discuss this week's Core Thoughts; that the gospel:
   a. of consumer Christianity is no gospel at all,
   b. places prayer before competence,
   c. values community above individualism,
   d. values patient endurance above impatient accomplishment,
   e. values humility above celebrity.
4. Allow members to briefly share any insights, questions, or illumination they have resulting from this week's daily readings and exercises.

Discovering the Discipline: Lectio Divina

5. Read aloud to your group the following regarding meditation.

> The biblical text is a witness to God revealing himself. This revelation is not simply a series of random oracles that illuminate momentary obscurities or guide us through perplexing circumstances. This text is God-revealing: God creating, God saving, God blessing. The text has a context and the context is huge, massive, comprehensive. St. Paul is staggered by it: "O the depth of the riches and wisdom and knowledge of God! How unsearchable are his judgments and how inscrutable his ways! (Romans 11:33)

Meditation is the aspect of spiritual reading that trains us to read Scripture as a connected, coherent whole, not a collection of inspired bits and pieces.

> This world of revelation is not only large, it is coherent—every thing is connected as in a living organism. A living God is revealing himself, and so if we are going to get it at all we must enter the large livingness of it. Meditation rehearses this largeness, enters into what is there, remembering all the aspects that have been dismembered in our disobedience, noticing the connections, realizing the congruencies, picking up the echoes. There is always more to anything, any word or sentence, than meets the eye; meditation enters into the large backgrounds that are not immediately visible, that we overlooked the first time around.[5]

Discussing the Discipline

6. As a group, share what you experienced this week as you engaged in the practice of meditating upon God's Word, using the method *Lectio Divina*.

---

5. Peterson, *Eat This Book*, 99–102.

7. What actions did God's Spirit prompt you to take as He spoke to you this week?

Experience the Life

8. Play the ETL Course DVD "Week 4: Rediscovering the Good Life."

Discussion Questions

9. As a group, discuss the ideas that Bill Hull introduced, and answer the question below.

   What is the life described in the Beatitudes that is commanded in the Sermon on the Mount, both hard and easy?

Close

10. Share matters for the community to pray about through the following week.

Pray to close the meeting.

WEEK 4

Rediscovering the Good Life Community Meeting

DAY SIX

In preparation for this week's meeting, you will have read and reflected upon each of the week's five Core Thoughts, recorded your thoughts and observations, and are ready to recite this week's memory verse to the group.

At This Week's Meeting

1. Open this session by asking God to help us to truly hear one another and to listen carefully for His voice in all that will be said.
2. Have each member take a turn reciting to the group this week's memory verse.
3. Discuss this week's Core Thoughts; that the good life:
   a. is a beatific life,
   b. emanates from good character,
   c. leads to greatness,
   d. leads to a good name,
   e. leads to the Good King.
4. Allow members to briefly share any insights, questions, or illumination they have resulting from this week's daily readings and exercises.

Discovering the Discipline: Lectio Divina

5. Read aloud to your group the following regarding meditation.

The classical practice of *Lectio Divina*—the prayerful reading of the Bible, the book Christians believe to be divinely inspired—is being rediscovered and renewed in our time. . . . In the monastic way of doing *Lectio Divina* we listen to how God is addressing us in a particular text of scripture. From this perspective there are no stages, ladders or steps in *Lectio Divina*, but rather there are four moments along the circumference of a circle. All the moments of the circle are joined to each other in a horizontal and interrelated pattern as well as to the center, which is the Spirit of God speaking to us through the text and in our hearts. To pay attention to any one of the four "moments" is to be in direct relationship to all the others. In this perspective, one may begin one's prayer at any "moment" along the circle, as well as moving easily from one "moment" to another, according to the inspiration of the Spirit. . . . The early monks read scripture aloud so they were actually listening to it. They would then choose a phrase, or a sentence at the most, that impressed them. They would sit with that sentence or phrase without thinking of stages or following some predetermined schema, but just listening, repeating slowly the same short text over and over again. . . . As they listened, they might perceive a new depth to the text or an expanding meaning. A particular insight might also be singularly appropriate for them in their particular life situation or for the events of the coming day. . . . The monks listened not so much to understand the text, not to conceptualize or analyze it, but just to hear it. And to hear it without any preconceived purpose of what they were going to do with it. . . .

Those who practice *Lectio Divina* in this way are already moving toward the fourth "moment" of this dynamic process leading to resting in God. In response to a new insight, they might be inclined to respond in thanksgiving or with interior movements of love, praise or gratitude. As this listening attitude stabilizes, they might experience moments of contemplative prayer in the strict sense, in which they are just present to God, or quietly engulfed in the divine presence. In this situation, one's attentiveness to God expands into the sheer awareness of [his] divine presence. . . . For the moment, we break through the veil of our own ways of thinking. The external word of God in scripture awakens us to the interior Word of God in our inmost being. . . . This leads to the faith experience of the living Christ and increases the practical love for others that flows from that relationship. . . . The ripe fruit of the regular practice of *Lectio Divina* is assimilating the word of God and being assimilated by it. It is a movement from conversation to communion. It also enables us to express our deep spiritual experience of union with God in words or symbols that are appropriate. There is thus a movement not only into silence, but from silence to expression.[6]

Discussing the Discipline

6. As a group, share what you experienced this week as you engaged in the practice of meditating upon God's Word, using the method *Lectio Divina*.

7. What actions did God's Spirit prompt you to take as He spoke to you this week?

6. "The Classical Practice of Lectio Divina by Thomas Keating," Contemplative Outreach Ltd., http://www.centeringprayer.com/lectio.htm, accessed 31 July 2007.

Experience the Life

8. Play the ETL Course DVD "Week 5: Renewing the Mind, Part 1."

Discussion Questions

9. As a group, discuss the ideas that Bill Hull introduced, and answer the question below.

   How has our culture's images and ideas influenced our notion of what the good life is? How could this influence be a real problem for Christians training to be Christ's disciples?

Close

10. Share matters for the community to pray about through the following week. Pray to close the meeting.

WEEK 5

Renewing the Mind, Part 1: Ideas
Community Meeting

DAY SIX

In preparation for this week's meeting, you will have read and reflected upon each of the week's five Core Thoughts, recorded your thoughts and observations, and are ready to recite this week's memory verses to the group.

At This Week's Meeting

1. Open this session by asking God to help us truly hear one another and to listen carefully for His voice in all that will be said.
2. Have each member take a turn reciting this week's memory verses to the group.
3. Discuss this week's Core Thoughts that:
   a. transformation begins with the renewing of the mind,
   b. we are called to renew our mind through training,
   c. the renewing of the mind begins with transforming its ideas, images, and feelings,
   d. the bondage of the mind begins with conforming its ideas, images, and feelings, and
   e. God renews our mind by dislodging false ideas and establishing new ideas.
4. Allow members to briefly share any insights, questions, or illumination they have resulting from this week's daily readings and exercises.

Discovering the Discipline: Lectio Divina

5. Read aloud to your group the following regarding meditation.

Man is created to praise, reverence, and serve God our Lord, and by this means to save his soul. All other things on the face of the earth are created for man to help him fulfill the end for which he is created. From this it follows that man is to use these things to the extent that they will help him to attain his end. Likewise, he must rid himself of them in so far as they prevent him from attaining it.

Therefore we must make ourselves indifferent to all created things, in so far as it is left to the choice of our free will and is not forbidden. Acting accordingly, for our part, we should not prefer health to sickness, riches to poverty, honor to dishonor, a long life to a short one, and so in all things we should desire and choose only those things which will best help us attain the end for which we are created.[7]

Discussing the Discipline

6. As a group, share what you experienced this week as you engaged in the practice of meditating upon God's Word, using the method *Lectio Divina*.

7. What actions did God's Spirit prompt you to take as He spoke to you this week?

---

7. Anthony Mottola, *Spiritual Exercises of St. Ignatius* (New York: Image, 1989), 47–48.

Experience the Life

8. Play the ETL Course DVD "Book One: Believe as Jesus Believed," "Week Six: Renewing the Mind, Part 2."

Discussion Questions

9. As a group, discuss the ideas that Bill Hull introduced, and answer the question below.

   How are our emotions unruly? What is the lesson God was teaching to Cain (and to us)?

Close

10. Share matters for the community to pray about through the following week. Pray to close the meeting.

WEEK 6

Renewing the Mind, Part 2: Emotions Community Meeting

DAY SIX

In preparation for this week's meeting, you will have read and reflected upon each of the week's five Core Thoughts, recorded your thoughts and observations, and are ready to recite this week's memory verses to the group.

At This Week's Meeting

1. Open this session by asking God to help us to truly hear one another and to listen carefully for Your voice in all that will be said.
2. Have each member take a turn reciting to the group this week's memory verse.
3. Discuss this week's Core Thoughts that:
   a. images power ideas,
   b. distorted images empower lies,
   c. God's Word transforms distorted images,
   d. renewing the mind transforms the emotions, and
   e. emotions are renewed by placing them in subjection to a renewed mind.
4. Allow members to briefly share any insights, questions, or illumination they have resulting from this week's daily readings and exercises.

Discovering the Discipline: Lectio Divina

5. Read aloud to your group the following regarding meditation.

In Christian meditation we seek to live the experience of Scripture. Alexander Whyte says, "You open your New Testament. . . . And, by your imagination, that moment you are one of Christ's disciples on the spot, and are at His feet. . . . with your imagination anointed with holy oil. . . . at one time, you are the publican; at another time, you are the prodigal. . . . at another time, you are Mary Magdalene; at another time, Peter in the porch."

As a practical aid in living the experience of Scripture, Ignatius of Loyola encourages us to apply all our senses to our task. We smell the sea. We hear the lap of water along the shore. We see the crowd. We feel the sun on our heads and the hunger pangs in our stomachs. We taste the salt in the air. We touch the hem of his garment. . . .

Remember, in Meditative Prayer God is always addressing our will. Christ confronts us and asks us to choose. Having heard his voice, we are to obey his word. It is this ethical call to repentance, to change, to obedience that most clearly distinguishes Christian meditation from its Eastern and secular counterparts. In Meditative Prayer there is no loss of identity, no merging with the cosmic consciousness, no fanciful astral travel. Rather, we are called to life-transforming obedience because we have encountered the living God of Abraham, Isaac, and Jacob. Christ is truly present among us to heal us, to forgive us, to change us, to empower us.

There is a technical word for what I have been describing, and it might be helpful for you to know it—*lectio divina* (divine reading). This is a kind of reading in which the mind descends into the heart and both are drawn into the love and goodness of God.[8]

8. Foster, *Prayer*, 148–149.

Discussing the Discipline

6. As a group, share what you experienced this week as you engaged in the practice of meditating upon God's Word, using the method *Lectio Divina*.

7. What actions did God's Spirit prompt you to take as He spoke to you this week?

Experience the Life

8. Play the ETL Course DVD "Week One: Led into Temptation."

Discussion Questions

9. As a group, discuss the ideas that Bill Hull introduced, and answer the question below.

   In what sense can Jesus' time of testing in the wilderness be a metaphor for the proper way to live our lives?

Close

10. Share matters for the community to pray about through the following week.

Pray to close the meeting.

ABOUT THE AUTHORS

BILL HULL's mission is to call the church to return to its disciple-making roots. He is a writer and discipleship evangelist calling the church to choose the life, a journey which Jesus called every disciple to pursue. This journey leads to a life of spiritual transformation and service. A veteran pastor, Bill has written ten books on this subject. In 1990 he founded T-NET International, a ministry devoted to transforming churches into disciple-making churches.

The core of Bill's writing is Jesus Christ, Disciplemaker; The Disciple-Making Pastor; and The Disciple-Making Church. He now spends his time helping leaders experience personal transformation so they can help transform their churches. He spends a significant amount of his time and energy helping churches embark on the Choose the Life Journey.

Bill and his wife, Jane, have been married thirty-seven years and are blessed to have two sons, a daughter-in-law, and a grandson. They live a not-so-quiet life in southern California.

PAUL MASCARELLA has served in local church ministry for more than twenty-five years as an associate pastor, minister of music, and worship director while holding an executive management position at a daily newspaper in Los Angeles, California. He is currently a mentor and lecturer at Londen Institute Graduate School of Ministry, and serves on the board of directors for Bill Hull Ministries. He holds bachelor of philosophy and master of theological studies degrees.

Paul and his wife, Denise, take pleasure in three children and two grandchildren. They reside in southern California.

ALSO BY BILL HULL

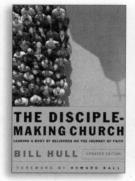

The Disciple-Making Pastor, rev. & exp. ed.

BakerBooks

The Disciple-Making Church, updated ed.

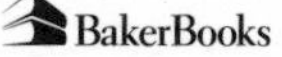

Jesus Christ, Disciplemaker, 20th ann. ed.

Choose the Life

Building High Commitment in a Low-Commitment World

Revell

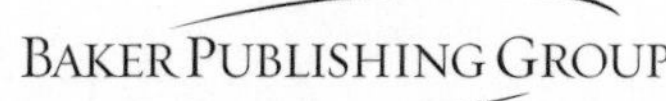

BAKER PUBLISHING GROUP

www.bakerpublishinggroup.com